CONCISE
LINCOLN
LIBRARY

—

EDITED BY RICHARD W. ETULAIN
AND SYLVIA FRANK RODRIGUE

CHRISTIAN G. SAMITO

Lincoln and the Thirteenth Amendment

Southern Illinois University Press
Carbondale

18 17 16 15 4 3 2 1

The Concise Lincoln Library has been made possible in part through a generous donation by the Leland E. and LaRita R. Boren Trust.

Jacket illustration adapted from a painting by Wendy Allen

Library of Congress Cataloging-in-Publication Data
Samito, Christian G.
Lincoln and the Thirteenth Amendment / Christian G. Samito.
pages cm. — (Concise Lincoln library)
Includes bibliographical references and index.
ISBN 978-0-8093-3424-7 (cloth : alk. paper)
ISBN 0-8093-3424-0 (cloth : alk. paper)
ISBN 978-0-8093-3425-4 (ebook)
ISBN 0-8093-3425-9 (ebook)
1. Lincoln, Abraham, 1809–1865—Views on slavery. 2. United States. Constitution. 13th Amendment—History. 3. United States—Politics and government—1861–1865. 4. Slaves—Emancipation—United States. I. Title.
E457.2.S27 2015
973.7092—dc23 2015000283

Printed on recycled paper. ♲
The paper used in this publication meets the minimum requirements of American National Standard for Information Sciences—Permanence of Paper for Printed Library Materials, ANSI Z39.48-1992. ∞

To an old friend who's given me
Lincolnian advice over the years,
Christopher M. Cesa

CONTENTS

ILLUSTRATIONS

LINCOLN AND THE THIRTEENTH AMENDMENT

INTRODUCTION

In his first public address after Congress passed a resolution proposing to the states a constitutional amendment to abolish slavery nationwide, President Abraham Lincoln called the measure "a King's cure for all the evils." For more than ten years, Lincoln had used medical analogies in speeches and debates when referring to slavery, likening it to a "wen or a cancer" that could not be cut out easily lest the patient "bleed to death." War had changed circumstances, however, so that on February 1, 1865, Lincoln now could identify a cure.[1]

Lincoln also took the opportunity to make a pun with a deeper meaning. Doctors at the time prescribed evening primrose oil, also commonly called King's cure-all, to remedy a variety of ailments. Lincoln had used the phrase "king-cure-all" once before, sarcastically, during an 1839 speech about the Democratic Party's plan for where to secure the nation's revenue. Lincoln now used the reference to acknowledge the complex and multifaceted nature of emancipation and to offer an optimistic opinion that the amendment would remedy the diverse problems caused by slavery.[2]

In hindsight, the amendment seems like an obvious means to accomplish a number of Lincoln's goals. Well before the Civil War, Lincoln had recognized the threat that bondage posed to the ideals of the Declaration of Independence at home and to the United States' reputation on the world stage. Moreover, Lincoln noted, slavery did more than endanger the principles imparted by the Founders; it challenged the very survival of the nation. As tension heightened in the

1850s, he asked, "Has any thing ever threatened the existence of this Union save and except this very institution of Slavery?" Morally, Lincoln had said of it, "If slavery is not wrong, nothing is wrong." The Thirteenth Amendment eliminated all of these threats and wrongs with slavery's immediate and nationwide abolition.[3]

Yet, the amendment actually broke with several of Lincoln's long-held prior positions. For most of his political career, Lincoln thought the Constitution should not be changed. Well into his presidency, Lincoln argued that emancipation could take place only on the state level because the federal government had no jurisdiction to control slavery where it existed in states. Additionally, Lincoln recognized the difficulties with emancipation on the ground, and accordingly, he favored gradual emancipation schemes as the best way to ease all Americans, white and black, toward the end of slavery. Regardless of whether one believes that Lincoln was serious about the idea (he in 1854 admitted its impracticality), his proposal of colonization for the freedpeople emphasized his concern that the transition from a slave society to an integrated one would prove difficult for all Americans.[4]

In other ways, however, the Thirteenth Amendment synchronized with some of Lincoln's long-held canons. By using the amendment process, Lincoln remained faithful to and worked within the Constitution, even while reforming it. Lincoln valued the will of the people, on which the amendment process relies, while the procedure outlined in the Constitution also moderated the threat that they could be impulsive decision makers. The amendment authorized Congress to enforce it with "appropriate legislation," which harmonized with Lincoln's view on the importance of the legislature, but this grant also maintained the separation of powers outlined in the Constitution because legislation is subject to presidential veto as well as to judicial review. Moreover, Lincoln saw in the amendment a way to shield federalism from the proposals of more radical Republicans. Amending the Constitution thus helped preserve one of its most important doctrines. Additionally, while Lincoln had to include the Confederate states in ratification so as to maintain consistency with his position that they had never seceded in the first place, doing so also fit with his generally lenient Reconstruction policy, and by giving white Southerners a voice in the process, he hoped to ease their hostility to abolition.

The story of Lincoln and the Thirteenth Amendment, then, is one of viewpoints regarding constitutional doctrine, political possibilities, ending the source of sectional division, and race relations reconsidered and transformed in the context of wartime. The Thirteenth Amendment set emancipation and Reconstruction on a path different from the one Lincoln had envisioned when he took office, with long-term implications that last to the present day. Moreover, the Thirteenth Amendment let some important questions remain open: What did freedom actually mean under its vague wording? How would its mechanics work? Luckily, one can find Lincoln's answers in the incomplete record he left upon his unexpected death.

In writing this book, I made an explicit choice not to reference the recent movie *Lincoln*. Through this book, readers can and will see for themselves what *Lincoln* got right, where it took liberties, and where it followed a historical source without interrogating its accuracy. Also, I have silently adjusted punctuation and capitalization to fit the text.

CHAPTER ONE

BEFORE THE PRESIDENCY

Abraham Lincoln opposed amending the Constitution during almost his entire political career. As a young politician in the 1830s and 1840s, as an emerging Republican leader in the 1850s, and even as president-elect during the winter of 1860–61, Lincoln adhered to several principles: a deep respect for the Constitution, a confidence that it could be interpreted within its boundaries to meet developments, and a belief he shared with most Americans that it should not be changed.

In January 1838, Lincoln, then a nearly twenty-nine-year-old member of the Illinois House of Representatives, coupled his veneration for the Constitution with a warning. Lincoln advised attendees of the Young Men's Lyceum of Springfield, Illinois, that if ever a "danger" threatened the Founders' creation, "it must spring up amongst us." No foreign invader could "take a drink from the Ohio, or make a track on the Blue Ridge, in a trial of a thousand years," Lincoln assured his listeners, but "if destruction be our lot, we must ourselves be its author and finisher."[1]

Lincoln then identified for his audience the "ill-omen" hovering over Jacksonian America: a marked increase in mob violence and "disregard for law" taking place in slave and free states alike. Lincoln argued that these events had ramifications broader than the harm suffered by the diverse groups—Catholics, black people, abolitionists, even gamblers—targeted in specific events. Mob violence inspired in ruffians disrespect for a government impotent to enforce its laws,

Lincoln warned, and in law-abiding citizens a feeling of disgust toward a government that failed to protect order through law. Lincoln feared that in the face of such chaos, "the strongest bulwark of any Government . . . may effectually be broken down and destroyed—I mean the *attachment* of the People."[2]

To solve the problem, Lincoln called for "reverence for the laws" to "become the political religion of the nation." Lincoln acknowledged that "bad laws" existed, but, he advised, "for the sake of example, they should be religiously observed" until their repeal. Lincoln concluded that "cold, calculating, unimpassioned reason" could be forged into the "intelligence," the "morality," and the "reverence for the constitution and laws" that would ensure the Republic's survival.[3]

Immediately upon his election as president, Lincoln faced the internal threat of disorder against which he warned—and on a scale larger than he ever imagined. A series of Southern states seceded from the United States and formed what Lincoln called a "giant insurrection," one that threatened the survival of the Founders' Union and Constitution. Even before he took the oath of office, some people called for amending the Constitution as a possible solution to the secession crisis, yet Lincoln did not like the idea. Instead, he hewed to a principle he had established years earlier: the Constitution should not be revised.[4]

In retrospect, it may seem surprising that Lincoln shunned the idea of constitutional amendment—after all, the Founders had included Article V as the means to change the Constitution they drafted. Yet even in the 1850s, when Lincoln challenged legal pronouncements such as the Kansas-Nebraska Act (1854) and Supreme Court chief justice Roger Taney's opinion in *Scott v. Sandford* (1857), he did not see constitutional amendment as the proper way to overturn laws with which he disagreed.

Political pragmatism might have guided Lincoln, who certainly realized that no constitutional amendment concerning such a divisive issue as slavery could be ratified by enough states to take effect. Decades earlier, then vice president John C. Calhoun of South Carolina had relied on this reality. Calhoun recognized the high bar involved—that three-fourths of the states had to ratify an amendment—when he argued that a state could nullify a federal law with which it disagreed, after which Congress could, if it chose to do so, invoke the Article V amendment process to resolve the controversy. Calhoun may have been writing about tariffs when he articulated this procedure in 1828, but he knew it could be used to safeguard slavery as well. Today, thirteen states can block an amendment proposed to the fifty states; when Calhoun wrote, twelve slave states existed in a Union of twenty-four, and by 1860, fifteen slave states could be found in a Union of thirty-three.[5]

Lincoln's stance regarding constitutional amendment went deeper, however. Years earlier, he had expressed his philosophical resistance to altering the document. President James K. Polk had repeatedly rejected legislation appropriating money for internal improvements, articulating in his veto messages the Democratic view that expenditures for that purpose fell outside the authority of the federal government. "I suppose an amendment to the Constitution, by consent of the States, necessary," Polk informed Congress in December 1847, quoting Thomas Jefferson, "because the objects now recommended are not among those enumerated in the Constitution, and to which it permits the public moneys to be applied."[6]

Several months later, Lincoln, as a first-term congressman, countered Polk's arguments; it was not the first speech Lincoln delivered on the House floor to oppose the president. After addressing other points Polk raised, Lincoln made his first recorded statement on amending the Constitution. "As a general rule, I think, we would do much better to let it alone," Lincoln advised, adding, "No slight occasion should tempt us to touch it." Lincoln further cautioned that taking "the first step . . . may lead to a habit of altering it. Better rather habituate ourselves to think of it as unalterable. It can scarcely be made better than it is. New provisions would introduce new difficulties, and thus create and increase appetite for still further change." Lincoln ended his point by asking, "New hands have never touched it. The men who made it have done their work, and have passed away. Who shall improve on what *they* did?"[7]

Lincoln believed, as did his Whig Party, that the federal government already had the constitutional authority to spend money on internal improvements. He also likely realized that supporting an amendment on that point would imply that such authority really did not exist. Yet, Lincoln did not argue that such an amendment would be superfluous. Instead, he affirmed his reverence for the nation's founding charter from which followed his near refusal to change it.

For Lincoln, as a Whig, issues were resolved properly by looking to the people's will as expressed through the legislature. As early as his 1836 reelection campaign for the Illinois state house, Lincoln promised, "While acting as [the people's] representative, I shall be governed by their will, on all subjects upon which I have the means of knowing what their will is; and upon all others, I shall do what my own judgment teaches me will best advance their interests." In Congress in July 1848, Lincoln said, "The people can elect whom they please, and afterwards, legislate just as they please, without any hindrance, save only so much as may guard against infractions of the constitution, undue haste, and want of consideration," and a few months later he urged a similar point in a speech to the Whig Club in Boston—in one local newspaper's paraphrase, that "the people's will should be obeyed, and not frustrated by Executive usurpation and the interposition of the veto power."[8]

During the 1850s, debate over slavery intensified, but not calls for constitutional change. By the 1830s, abolitionists rarely suggested using constitutional amendment to end bondage. Representative John Quincy Adams of Massachusetts, a former president, did so in 1839, proposing amendments to forbid the admission of any more slave states to the Union, to end slavery in Washington, D.C., as of July 4, 1845, and to hold as free every child born in the United States after July 4, 1842. The House of Representatives could not consider Adams's plan, however, due to its self-imposed gag rule on discussing the topic of slavery. No member of Congress would again propose an antislavery amendment until after the Civil War began.[9]

Slaveholders in the 1850s recognized the long-term threat Article V posed to their institution unless it could expand. If antislavery forces managed to keep slavery out of the vast western territories, possibly enough free states could be carved from them to join the already existing free states in ratifying an antislavery constitutional amendment. Republican opposition to slavery and Lincoln's election in 1860 provided reminders of this possibility. Yet, like the abolitionists, slaveholders did not see constitutional amendment as a viable option either. In 1850 Representative John R. J. Daniel of North Carolina raised the idea of amending Article V to prohibit any amendment to abolish or affect slavery in any state without the concurrence of all states where slavery existed, but his proposal ended after a colleague objected on a procedural point. Radicals in South Carolina devised a different protection against antislavery amendments: they expanded Calhoun's nullification doctrine to argue that if a state rejected an amendment ultimately ratified by three-fourths of the states, the rejecting state could either imply its consent by remaining in the Union or it could withdraw.[10]

Lincoln thus shared in a general consensus of Americans in the decade prior to the Civil War that the Constitution should not be amended. When Lincoln declared at an August 1856 Republican rally that Democrats sought to put the government "on a new track" and make slavery its "ruling element," he finished his speech with an admonition, "Don't interfere with anything in the Constitution. That must be maintained, for it is the only safeguard of our liberties." Lincoln—and most Americans—viewed constitutionalism as a matter of properly interpreting the document, not revising it, with guidance from the Founders. As Lincoln said at the Cooper Institute in February 1860, "I do not mean to say we are bound to follow implicitly in whatever our fathers did. To do so, would be to discard all the lights of current experience—to reject all progress—all improvement. What I do say is, that if we would supplant the opinions and policy of our fathers in any case, we should do so upon evidence so conclusive, and argument so clear, that even their great authority, fairly considered and weighed, cannot stand."[11]

Making sense of why Lincoln took the positions he did in the 1850s is made easier if one recognizes that he would not consider amending the Constitution but wanted to work within its framework as he understood it. In Chicago in July 1858, Lincoln said of slavery, "In the States where it exists we have no right to interfere with it because it is in the Constitution and we are by both duty and inclination to stick by that Constitution in all its letter and spirit from beginning to end." Lincoln had held this viewpoint for decades: in 1837, the young state legislator signed a protest against an anti-abolitionist resolution passed by the Illinois legislature in which he assured of his belief that "Congress . . . has no power, under the constitution, to interfere with the institution of slavery in the different States."[12]

Lincoln's interpretation was conventional. In 1790, the House of Representatives had adopted a report that held, in part, "Congress have no authority to interfere in the emancipation of slaves, or in the treatment of them within any of the States; it remaining with the several States alone to provide any regulations therein." Since that time, nearly every constitutional thinker understood that the states determined matters of slavery and freedom and even many of the rights and privileges now associated with national citizenship.[13]

Lincoln believed elections were the proper way for the people to declare their will regarding slavery and other issues. In the aftermath of John Brown's raid on Harpers Ferry, Lincoln in December 1859 observed, "We have a means provided for the expression of our belief in regard to Slavery—it is through the ballot box—the peaceful method provided by the Constitution." Through elections, the people chose their presidents, legislators, and, in an indirect way, members of the Supreme Court. Yet, Lincoln's reading of the Constitution also restricted the scope of the people's ability to declare their will because interpretation reached only so far. No matter what his personal views on slavery, Lincoln faced constraints if, according to his constitutionalism, the federal government could not touch it in the states where it existed. Under Lincoln's view, the federal government could prohibit slavery only in the territories. When one recognizes that Lincoln had eliminated the possibility of amending the Constitution, held a deep commitment to adhering to it, and believed that it prevented the federal government from interfering with slavery in the states where it existed, it becomes clearer that for Lincoln, no other antislavery agenda was open to him except for congressional legislation prohibiting the expansion of slavery. This position also fit with Lincoln's generally moderate tone, and it held greater political appeal and viability than more radical propositions.[14]

Thus, in Peoria, Illinois, in October 1854, Lincoln could call slavery a "monstrous injustice" and declare his hatred of it for violating the Declaration of Independence. Lincoln noted that it tainted as hypocritical America's global reputation and created the antithesis of American democracy: "When the white man governs himself that is self-government; but when he governs himself, and also governs *another* man, that is *more* than self-government—that is despotism." Lincoln also observed how slaveholding curtailed the free speech and other rights of many white Americans, rendering them "deprived of the privilege of governing themselves as they would, by the action of a very few, in the beginning." At the same time, however, Lincoln felt that the only constitutional way he could try to put slavery on a path to extinction was to prevent its expansion. To accomplish this goal, he and other Republicans turned to Article IV, Section 3 of the Constitution, which stated, "The Congress shall have Power to dispose of and make all needful Rules and Regulations respecting the Territory . . . belonging to the United States."[15]

Lincoln and other Republicans expected that excluding slavery from territories would ensure their eventual entry into the Union as free states because they would contain no slaveholders. While more radical Republicans called for stronger measures, moderate Republicans like Lincoln felt hemming slavery in, and hoping it would eventually wither and die, was the best they could do to attack bondage in the states where it already existed. As Lincoln said in one of his debates with Stephen Douglas, one may not be able to cut out a cancer from his body lest he bleed to death, "but surely it is no way to cure it, to engraft it and spread it over your whole body." For Lincoln, "the fathers themselves set us the example" of "restricting the spread" of slavery. This moderate policy had the added political advantage of allowing its proponents, like Lincoln, to cast themselves as conservatives simply trying to maintain the Founders' vision of government in the face of slaveholders' efforts to disregard it.[16]

In 1857 Chief Justice Roger Taney jeopardized the Republican agenda concerning slavery in the territories. In his opinion in the *Dred Scott* case, Taney held that black people could not be U.S. citizens. Going beyond what the Supreme Court had jurisdiction to address, Taney further maintained that Congress could not prohibit slavery in territory gained after enactment of the Constitution despite the broad language of Article IV, Section 3. Taney stated that even a change in "public opinion or feeling, in relation to this unfortunate race," could not "induce the court to give to the words of the Constitution a more liberal construction in their favor than they were intended to bear when the instrument was framed and adopted." The chief justice signaled a way to overcome his ruling, though: "If any of its provisions are deemed unjust, there is a mode prescribed in the instrument itself by which it may be amended; but while it remains unaltered, it must be construed now as it was understood at the time of its adoption."[17]

Taney held as unconstitutional the critical point on which Republicans like Lincoln hoped to rely: congressional prohibition of slavery in the territories. Yet, despite Taney's reference to Article V, neither Lincoln nor the Republican Party discussed such a constitutional amendment in response to the *Dred Scott* case. In June 1857 Lincoln assured of his "respect for the judicial department of government" and belief that "its decisions on Constitutional questions, when fully settled, should control, not only the particular cases decided, but the general policy of the country, subject to be disturbed only by amendments of the Constitution as provided in that instrument itself." Lincoln warned that to do "more than this would be revolution," yet he did not propose amending the Constitution. Instead, he attacked Taney's opinion as "erroneous" and, noting that the Court had overruled itself in the past, vowed, "We shall do what we can to have it to over-rule this." Lincoln went on to say that the errors on which Taney based his decision, the fact that the Supreme Court had not repeatedly affirmed in a series of cases the principles Taney expressed, and the reality that a large part of the public felt dissatisfied with the ruling meant "it is not resistance, it is not factious, it is not even disrespectful, to treat it as not having yet quite established a settled doctrine for the country." Lincoln saw the American people, not the Court, as the final arbiter of constitutional decisions. For Lincoln, however, that process did not involve amendment but decisions at the ballot box resulting in, among other things, the appointment of judges who eventually would overturn a questionable ruling.[18]

Shortly before engaging in his famous series of debates with Stephen Douglas, Lincoln reaffirmed his position that no amendment was necessary regarding *Dred Scott*. In a speech in July 1858, Lincoln noted how Democrats had rejected the Supreme Court's holding in *McCulloch v. Maryland* (1819). Even though the Court had unanimously ruled that Congress could charter a Bank of the United States, Democratic president Andrew Jackson vetoed its recharter in 1832. Lincoln now challenged Douglas, "Will you not graciously allow us to do with the Dred Scott decision precisely as you did with the Bank decision? You succeeded in breaking down the moral effect of that decision; did you find it necessary to amend the Constitution?"[19]

The *Dred Scott* ruling shows how a Supreme Court decision can galvanize democratic debate about an issue. Lincoln lost the Senate election to Douglas, but in the process he became a rising Republican leader. Over a year later, Lincoln articulated his agenda in a speech in Cincinnati, Ohio: "We must not interfere with the institution of slavery in the states where it exists, because the constitution forbids it, and the general welfare does not require us to do so," Lincoln affirmed, "[b]ut we must prevent the outspreading of the institution, because neither the constitution nor general welfare requires us to extent [*sic*] it." Lincoln next turned to how to implement his plan. After he had reminded his audience that "the people of these United States are the rightful masters of both Congresses and courts not to overthrow the constitution, but to overthrow the men who pervert that constitution," Lincoln announced, "We must hold conventions; we must adopt platforms if we conform to ordinary custom; we must nominate candidates, and we must carry elections."[20]

Yet, nowhere did Lincoln say, "We must amend the Constitution." Lincoln spoke of the will of the people—he reminded Illinois Republicans in December 1856, after the defeat of their presidential candidate, John C. Frémont, that "our government rests on public opinion," and he acknowledged that Republicans could help shape those views—but he also consistently declined to support constitutional amendment as a way for the people to express their will. George Washington may have noted in his 1796 Farewell Address that the Founding generation had refined the Lockean right to change government into a peaceful, political process: "The basis of our political systems is the right of the people to make and to alter their constitutions of government." Lincoln, however, would have focused on the final phrase of Washington's next sentence: "But the constitution which at any time exists till changed by an explicit and authentic act of the whole people is sacredly obligatory upon all."[21]

CHAPTER TWO

SECESSION WINTER

In 1860 Lincoln ran for president on a Republican platform that handled slavery exactly as he had proposed during the preceding decade: the federal government could not interfere with slavery in the states where it existed but should oppose its expansion in any of the territories. Almost immediately after Lincoln's election on this platform came threats of disunion. Slaveholders and other sympathetic white Southerners recognized that besides hemming slavery in, a Republican president would try to build his party in the South with the use of patronage. Moreover, they feared, he might take steps to safeguard delivery of antislavery tracts through the postal service, challenging one of the means—censoring the mail—used by slavery's supporters to prevent discussion of the issue. On November 10, 1860, South Carolina's legislature called for a special convention to consider secession. The 1850s had been a quiet time for amendment ideas—the only such change proposed in Congress between January 1854 and the time of Lincoln's election came in January 1858, and it addressed voter qualifications in the election of representatives. After Lincoln's election, however, came dozens of calls to amend the Constitution.[1]

President James Buchanan initiated the discussion with an amendment proposal in the Annual Message he sent to Congress on December 3, 1860. Buchanan sought an amendment recognizing the right of property in slaves in the states where bondage existed or may thereafter exist and the "duty" of protecting this right in all the territories until they should be admitted as states into the Union with or without slavery, as their constitutions may prescribe. Buchanan also called for this amendment to affirm the right of owners to have their escaped slaves restored to them and for all state laws impairing that right to be held null and void. Buchanan explained, "It may be objected that this construction of the Constitution has already been settled by the Supreme Court of the United States, and what more ought to be required? The answer is, that a very large proportion of the people of the United States still contest the correctness of this decision, and never will cease from agitation and admit its binding force until clearly established by the people of the several States in their sovereign character." Buchanan believed "an explanatory amendment" would "restore peace and harmony among the States."[2]

Lincoln maintained a public silence lest he say something to antagonize proslavery advocates, antislavery forces, or members of both groups. Moreover, as Lincoln explained to Representative John A. Gilmer of North Carolina, his positions were "all in print and easy of access," and he feared any public statement now would be used to "make me appear as if I repented for the crime of having been elected, and was anxious to apologize and beg forgiveness."[3]

Privately, however, the president-elect made known his position to several Republican members of Illinois' congressional delegation, abandoning his Whiggish deference to the legislature to become a voice in its discussion. On December 10, 1860, he wrote to Senator Lyman Trumbull, "Let there be no compromise on the question of extending slavery. If there be, all our labor is lost, and, ere long, must be done again." Noting that some Republicans may waver in the face of threats of secession, Lincoln urged Trumbull, "Have none of it. Stand firm. The tug has to come, & better now, than any time hereafter." Lincoln followed this message by sending Representative William Kellogg (who represented Illinois on the Committee of Thirty-Three formed by the House of Representatives to address the disunion crisis) and Representative Elihu B. Washburne letters nearly identical to the one he sent Trumbull. Regarding the extension of slavery, Lincoln added to Washburne, "On that point hold firm, as with a chain of steel," and regarding the Fugitive Slave Act, Lincoln told Kellogg, "You know I think the fugitive slave clause of the constitution ought to be enforced—to put it on the mildest form, ought not to be resisted." Lincoln marked all three letters confidential to prevent their publication but assumed the recipients would convey their message to other Republicans. On December 17, Lincoln wrote another confidential letter to Trumbull in which he advised, "If any of our friends do prove false, and fix up a compromise on the territorial question, I am for fighting again—that is all," and added, "It is but repetition for me to say I am for an honest inforcement [*sic*] of the constitution—fugitive slave clause included." Lincoln reiterated the point in February 1861, though he admitted he could overlook expansion in New Mexico territory, allowed by the Compromise of 1850 to determine for itself whether to permit slavery, so long as no further enlargement of slavery took place.[4]

Lincoln also turned to filling his cabinet. On December 8, 1860, he offered Senator William H. Seward of New York the position of secretary of state. On December 11 Seward's advisor Thurlow Weed, an influential Republican in his own right, wrote Lincoln to ask his "views upon vital questions," and shortly after he began a trip to confer with the president-elect in Illinois. Lincoln responded to Weed's letter that he would be "inflexible on the territorial question" and offered only the suggestion, "I probably think all opposition, real and apparant [*sic*], to the fugitive slave [clause] of the constitution ought to be withdrawn," adding, "It is the duty of the President, and other government functionaries to run the machine as it is." Lincoln remained consistent to the idea of working within the Constitution.[5]

On December 20 South Carolina made the crisis real when its special convention voted to secede. Two days earlier the Senate had formed the Committee of Thirteen, in addition to the House Committee of Thirty-Three, to try to agree on a "general plan of adjustment." That same day, Senator John Crittenden of Kentucky proposed a package of six constitutional amendments aimed at keeping the slave states in the Union: (1) slavery would be prohibited in territory north of the Missouri Compromise line and recognized in territory south of it, with states admitted to the Union with or without slavery as their constitutions provided; (2) Congress could not abolish slavery in places under its jurisdiction within a slave state, for example military posts; (3) Congress could not abolish slavery in the District of Columbia as long as it existed in the adjoining states of Virginia and Maryland and without the consent of the District's inhabitants, with compensation to slave owners who did not consent to abolition; (4) Congress could not prohibit or interfere with the interstate slave trade; (5) the federal government would compensate owners of fugitive slaves and try to recover payment by suing the county in which obstruction to the fugitive slave laws took place (the county, in turn, could sue individuals who obstructed return of fugitive slaves); and (6) no future amendment of the Constitution could change these amendments or authorize Congress to interfere with slavery within any slave state. On the motion of Senator Jefferson Davis of Mississippi, the Committee of Thirteen agreed not to report any proposal unless a majority of Republicans and a majority of Democrats on the committee supported it. That proved not possible, and on December 31, 1860, the committee reported to the Senate that it could not agree to any plan, Crittenden's included. Members of Congress continued to discuss Crittenden's compromise proposal, but the inaction of the committee effectively killed it.[6]

Lincoln, meanwhile, drew up resolutions of his own for the Senate to consider. On December 20 the president-elect met with Weed in Springfield, Illinois, and gave him three written propositions for Seward to introduce to the Committee of Thirteen on which he served. Lincoln's resolutions read: (1) "That the fugitive slave clause of the Constitution ought to be enforced by a law of Congress, with efficient provisions for that object, not obliging private persons to assist in it's [*sic*] execution, but punishing all who resist it, and with the usual safeguards to liberty, securing free men against being surrendered as slaves"; (2) "That all state laws, if there be such, really, or apparantly [*sic*], in conflict with such law of Congress, ought to be repealed; and no opposition to the execution of such law of Congress ought to be made"; and (3) "That the Federal Union must be preserved." Lincoln noted the next day in a letter to Lyman Trumbull that he expressly avoided addressing the territorial question.[7]

Weed subsequently conferred with Seward aboard a train as the senator traveled from upstate New York to the nation's capital. Seward later reported to Lincoln that during this meeting, Weed gave him "verbally the substance of the suggestion you proposed for the consideration of the Republican members, but not the written proposition." On December 24 Seward met first with the Republican members of the Committee of Thirteen and then the entire committee; he later reported to Lincoln that "with the unanimous consent of our section I offered three propositions which seemed to me to cover the ground of the suggestion made by you through Mr[.] Weed as I understood it."[8]

Seward actually went beyond Lincoln's instructions. Where Lincoln had called for several congressional resolutions and nowhere mentioned revising the Constitution, Seward proposed a package of constitutional amendments holding that (1) no amendment should be made to the Constitution to authorize Congress to abolish or interfere with slavery in the states; (2) the fugitive slave law should be amended to grant fugitives a jury trial; and (3) state legislatures should review their applicable law codes and repeal or modify any legislation that contravened the Constitution regarding the "right of persons recently resident in other States." The committee approved the first proposition (which Lincoln did not suggest in the document he gave Weed) and rejected the other two (which Lincoln did suggest).[9]

Seward here substituted his judgment for that of Lincoln's, hoping, perhaps, with his proposal to rebut secessionist propaganda and thus strengthen unionism in the Upper South. Secession commissioners had already warned the slave states that had not yet seceded that the Republicans would ignore the Constitution. William L. Harris of Mississippi told the Georgia General Assembly, for instance, that the Constitution now stood "broken and overturned," and to the Virginia convention considering secession, Henry L. Benning of Georgia cautioned that the North was on its way to "acquiring the power to abolish slavery" through constitutional amendment.[10]

Another possibility is that Weed verbally miscommunicated the president-elect's wishes to Seward or that Seward misunderstood what Weed had told him. Seward afterward perhaps sought some cover when he wrote Lincoln on December 26, 1860, that he had received from Weed the written copy of Lincoln's proposed resolutions only that morning. Seward's letter also made clear that he understood that he had deviated from Lincoln's document: he informed Lincoln that the Republican members of the committee, along with Senators Trumbull of Illinois and William Pitt Fessenden of Maine, planned to meet that evening at his home "to consider your written suggestion and determine whether it shall be offered." Seward added, "While we think the ground has been already covered we find that in the form you give it[,] it would divide our friends not only in the Committee but in Congress[,] a portion being unwilling to give up their old opinion that the duty of executing the constitutional provisions concerning fugitives from service belongs to the States, and not at all to Congress." Two days later, Seward accepted Lincoln's nomination as secretary of state; he did not, however, submit Lincoln's proposed resolutions to the Committee of Thirteen, which adjourned on the final day of 1860.[11]

In these closing days of the year, Duff Green, a newspaper publisher, diplomat, and acquaintance of Lincoln's, visited the president-elect at Buchanan's request. Green arrived in Springfield, Illinois, hoping to obtain a letter from Lincoln that would reassure the South. In response, Lincoln provided a letter to Lyman Trumbull with instructions to give it to Green or withhold delivery of the letter "if, on consultation with our discreet friends, you conclude that it may do us harm." Lincoln wrote in the letter for Green, "I do not desire any amendment of the Constitution," but he acknowledged that, because "questions of such amendment rightfully belong to the American People, I should not feel justified, nor inclined, to withhold from them, if I could, a fair opportunity of expressing their will thereon, through either of the modes prescribed in the instrument." Lincoln affirmed in the letter to Green his opinion that "the right of each state to order and control its own domestic institutions according to its own judgment exclusively, is essential to that balance of powers on which the perfection, and endurance of our political fabric depends—and I denounce the lawless invasion, by armed force, of the soil of any State or Territory, no matter under what pretext, as the gravest of crimes." Lincoln consented to publication of the letter to Green only if six of the twelve U.S. senators from Georgia, Alabama, Mississippi, Louisiana, Florida, and Texas signed their names below a statement written on it underneath the president-elect's signature, "We recommend to the people of the States we represent respectively, to suspend all action for dismemberment of the Union, at least, until some act, deemed to be violative of our rights, shall be done by the incoming administration," and allowed the entire document to be published as a whole.[12]

Trumbull decided not to circulate the letter, though he probably showed it to Green at least by January 7, 1861. The next day, the *New York Herald* published Green's account in which he stated he was convinced that Lincoln would "administer the government in such a manner as to satisfy the South." Green likely wrote this statement before seeing Lincoln's letter, because on January 7 he wrote the president-elect, "I regret your unwillingness to recommend an amendment to the constitution which will arrest the progress of secession."[13]

On the other hand, in a subtle way, Lincoln did indicate a willingness to consider amendments. On January 12, 1861, Seward delivered a lengthy and conciliatory speech in the Senate in which he stated that slavery existing in any state "is wisely left by the Constitution of the United States exclusively to the care, management, and disposition of that State; and if it were in my power, I would not alter the Constitution in that respect." Seward added, moreover, a version of the amendment he had proposed in the Committee of Thirteen: "I am willing to vote for an amendment of the Constitution, declaring that it shall not, by any future amendment, be so altered as to confer on Congress a power to abolish or interfere with slavery in any State." Later in his speech, Seward proposed "a convention of the people," after passions had cooled, "to consider and decide whether any and what amendments of the organic national law ought to be made." Seward added that he adhered to "the principle that this Government exists in its present form only by the consent of the governed, and that it is as necessary as it is wise, to resort to the people for revisions of the organic law when the troubles and dangers of the State certainly transcend the powers delegated by it to the public authorities." Of the government, Seward stated, "Perfect as it is, it ought to be expected that it will, at least as often as once in a century, require some modification to adapt it to the changes of society and alternations of empire."[14]

A week later, Lincoln wrote Seward in a private letter, "Your recent speech is well received here; and, I think, is doing good all over the country." Lincoln did not admonish Seward for any of his amendment proposals, perhaps sensing that the time for compromise had passed anyway. No amendment could be ratified by enough states at this point, and such discussion at least made the Republicans look reasonable and willing to keep open a dialogue. In light of their futility, what good would it do to chastise his new secretary of state for proposing constitutional amendments?[15]

A less appealing possibility, from an antislavery standpoint, is that Lincoln had changed course to support tacitly a constitutional amendment such as Seward suggested. Lincoln had, after all, run on a platform that the federal government had no power to interfere with slavery in the states. However, this alternative seems highly unlikely. Lincoln had long expressed a hesitance to amending the Constitution in the first place. In the letter he drafted for Duff Green, Lincoln reiterated his personal opposition to changing the founding charter—the most he could bring himself to do in that letter was acknowledge that the will of the American people governed on the matter. Moreover, it is hard to imagine Lincoln supporting a change to the Constitution to include written protection for slavery. Lincoln, in October 1854, had argued that the Founders tolerated slavery because they had to do so—he observed that "they forbore to so much as mention the word 'slave' or 'slavery' in the whole instrument" and "the thing is hid away, in the constitution, just as an afflicted man hides away a wen or a cancer." Lincoln argued that "necessity drove them so far, and farther, they would not go." Would Lincoln now go farther than they?[16]

Yet, Lincoln also affirmed his Whiggish deference to Congress in a speech in Pittsburgh in mid-February 1861 that focused on tariff policy. "According to my political education," Lincoln announced, "I am inclined to believe that the people in the various sections of the country should have their own views carried out through their representatives in Congress." Lincoln's manuscript for the speech contained some additional language he does not seem to have used: "By the constitution, the executive may recommend measures which he may think proper; and he may veto those he thinks improper; and it is supposed he may add to these, certain indirect influences to affect the action of congress. My political education strongly inclines me against a very free use of any of these means, by the Executive, to control the legislation of the country. As a rule, I think it better that congress should originate, as well as perfect its measures, without external bias."[17]

An amendment, however, *did* get reported out of Congress: a possible Thirteenth Amendment far different from the one passed and ratified in 1865. Seward's friend Charles Francis Adams proposed to the House's Committee of Thirty-Three an amendment very similar to the first one Seward had proposed to the Senate's counterpart Committee of Thirteen. The chair of the House committee, Thomas Corwin of Ohio, reported the amendment in January 1861, and thus it is sometimes identified as the Corwin Amendment. The amendment's association with Seward, who also lobbied for it, has led some historians erroneously to think that Lincoln supported the measure. For the reasons discussed in the preceding paragraphs, that seems unlikely. At first, Republicans opposed the amendment, but gradually some of them changed course, believing the amendment might cripple the secession movement by preserving the allegiance of slaveholding states that had not yet seceded. Additionally, some people interpreted Seward's support for the measure as that of Lincoln's as well. The Corwin Amendment passed the House on February 28, 1861, and the Senate three days later. It read: "No amendment shall be made to the Constitution which will authorize or give to Congress the power to abolish, or interfere, within any State, with the domestic institutions thereof, including that of persons held to labor or service by the laws of said State." In one of his last official acts, Buchanan signed the measure, even though Article V does not require a presidential signature on a proposed amendment. Ohio ratified the amendment on May 13, 1861, although by then Fort Sumter had made it a moot point. Maryland did so as well on January 10, 1862.[18]

On March 4—the day after the Senate approved the Corwin Amendment—Lincoln took the oath of office. In his Inaugural Address, Lincoln reiterated his position that he had "no purpose, directly or indirectly, to interfere with the institution of slavery in the States where it exists. I believe I have no lawful right to do so, and I have no inclination to do so," and he quoted applicable language from the 1860 Republican platform. Lincoln then announced a policy he articulated back in 1838, before the Young Men's Lyceum of Springfield: "While I do not choose now to specify particular acts of Congress as proper to be enforced, I do suggest, that it will be much safer for all, both in official and private stations, to conform to, and abide by, all those acts which stand unrepealed, than to violate any of them."[19]

Lincoln coupled his duty to follow the Constitution with his recognition of the power of the will of the people: "I shall take care, as the Constitution itself expressly enjoins upon me, that the laws of the Union be faithfully executed in all the States. Doing this I deem to be only a simple duty on my part; and I shall perform it, so far as practicable, unless my rightful masters, the American people, shall withhold the requisite means, or, in some authoritative manner, direct the contrary." At the same time, Lincoln admitted that controversies involving interpretation would arise: "No organic law can ever be framed with a provision specifically applicable to every question which may occur in practical administration." Lincoln provided some relevant examples: "Shall fugitives from labor be surrendered by national or by State authority? The Constitution does not expressly say. *May* Congress prohibit slavery in the territories? The Constitution does not expressly say. *Must* Congress protect slavery in the territories? The Constitution does not expressly say."[20]

Lincoln next tied the will of the people into his thoughts regarding the proper role of the Supreme Court. While accepting that its decisions were binding upon the parties to a suit and "entitled to very high respect and consideration, in all paralel [*sic*] cases, by all other departments of the government," Lincoln also announced, "The candid citizen must confess that if the policy of the government, upon vital questions, affecting the whole people, is to be irrevocably fixed by decisions of the Supreme Court, the instant they are made, in ordinary litigation between parties, in personal actions, the people will have ceased, to be their own rulers, having, to that extent, practically resigned their government, into the hands of that eminent tribunal. Nor is there, in this view, any assault upon the court, or the judges."[21]

Toward the end of his speech, Lincoln coupled his thoughts on amending the Constitution in general with the role of the will of the people. The new president stated, "This country, with its institutions, belongs to the people who inhabit it. Whenever they shall grow weary of the existing government, they can exercise their *constitutional* right of amending it, or their *revolutionary* right to dismember, or overthrow it." Lincoln acknowledged, "While I make no recommendation of amendments, I fully recognize the rightful authority of the people over the whole subject, to be exercised in either of the modes prescribed in the instrument itself; and I should, under existing circumstances, favor, rather than oppose, a fair oppertunity [*sic*] being afforded the people to act upon it."[22]

Lincoln then made a surprising break with his prior political thought: he advised use of a clause of Article V never actually implemented before 1861 or since, that Congress, "on the Application of the Legislatures of two thirds of the several States, shall call a Convention for proposing Amendments." Lincoln declared that, in his opinion, "the convention mode seems preferable, in that it allows amendments to originate with the people themselves, instead of only permitting them to take, or reject, propositions, originated by others, not especially chosen for the purpose, and which might not be precisely such, as they would wish to either accept or refuse." Previously, Lincoln had deferred to Congress as the voice of the people's will; now, he looked to the convention method as an even better vehicle for that purpose, and he advised the convening of a miniature constitutional convention. Under this method, delegates would be elected to address a specific issue or set of issues, under the assumption that this specially elected convention would be a more direct agent of the people, and better able to express their will on the topics at hand, than would be the legislature.[23]

Lincoln probably uttered these words in his Inaugural Address with great internal hesitation as well as the realization they would come to naught; he likely did so in the hope the sentiment would make him look moderate. Lincoln's draft inaugural contained a very different statement from the one he made on March 4, 1861. In Lincoln's draft, the relevant paragraph started similarly enough—"This country, with its institutions, belongs to the people who inhabit it. Whenever they shall grow weary of the existing government, they can exercise their constitutional right of amending it, or their revolutionary right to dismember or overthrow it"—but continued, "As I am not much impressed with the belief that the present Constitution can be improved, I make no recommendations of amendments. I am, rather, for the old ship, and the chart of the old pilots. If, however, the people desire a new, or an altered vessel, the matter is exclusively their own, and they can move in the premises, as well without as with an executive recommendation. I shall place no obstacle in the way of what may appear to be their wishes." Seward suggested striking the sentence "As I am not much impressed . . ." and replacing it with "While so great a diversity of opinion exists on the question what amendments, if, indeed any would be effective in restoring peace and safety, it would only tend to aggravate the dispute if I were to attempt to give direction to the public mind in that respect." Lincoln rejected Seward's proposed language.[24]

Lincoln also addressed the Corwin Amendment in his Inaugural Address: "I understand a proposed amendment to the Constitution—which amendment, however, I have not seen, has passed Congress, to the effect that the federal government, shall never interfere with the domestic institutions of the States, including that of persons held to service. To avoid misconstruction of what I have said, I depart from my purpose not to speak of particular amendments, so far as to say that, holding such a provision to now be implied constitutional law, I have no objection to its being made express, and irrevocable." Here, then, Lincoln issued his tepid and politically expedient endorsement of a proposal that comported with constitutional procedure and deference to the will of the people. Lincoln likely realized the measure had no chance of being ratified but could be used to allay the fears of undecided Southerners. At this point, the Upper South—North Carolina, Virginia, Arkansas, Tennessee, Maryland, Delaware, Kentucky, and Missouri—had not yet seceded, and whether they would do so hung in the balance.

The first four states would secede; the rest remained in the Union and are referred to as the Border States.[25]

On March 16, 1861, Lincoln dutifully sent a form letter to all the governors of the states, including those that claimed to have seceded, in which he enclosed "an authenticated copy of a Joint Resolution to amend the Constitution of the United States adopted by Congress and approved . . . by James Buchanan, President." The new president followed the law even though he did not approve of amending the Constitution in general, nor did he like the specific proposal at hand. Nonetheless, Lincoln sent it for the people to judge through the ratification process, and he carefully gave no endorsement of the measure, instead making sure to highlight that his predecessor had signed the resolution, not him.[26]

CHAPTER THREE

TOWARD THE EMANCIPATION PROCLAMATION

By the time he took office, Lincoln had for decades proclaimed that the federal government could not interfere with slavery in states where it existed. This position, however, did not forbid the federal government from trying to induce states to abolish slavery on their own. Early in his presidency, Lincoln sought to convince the Border States to do just that and thus eliminate hope in the Confederacy that any of them would join it. Lincoln wanted to encourage state legislatures to end slavery gradually within their jurisdictions by offering federal compensation in exchange for emancipation. Gradual, state-based emancipation had long been a historical feature in the United States, so it is no surprise Lincoln would have thought in this way. As British colonies, all the states had slavery in them. During the Revolution and the years that followed, the northern states abolished bondage, but most of them had emancipated their slaves gradually.

Lincoln, as a careful constitutional thinker, also had concerns that the Fifth Amendment's prohibition that no person shall be "deprived of life, liberty, or property, without due process of law," could be used to make arguments to prevent emancipation without compensation in the loyal states. Chief Justice Taney had explicitly raised Fifth Amendment protection in his opinion in the *Dred Scott* case: "An act of Congress which deprives a citizen of the United States of his liberty or property, merely because he came himself or brought his property into a particular Territory of the United States . . . could hardly be dignified with the name of due process of law." Compensated emancipation, however, eliminated any such concern and precluded any argument that could be crafted from the Takings Clause in the Fifth Amendment, "nor shall private property be taken for public use without just compensation." Finally, gradual and compensated emancipation was politically expedient: it showed Lincoln's desire to work toward slavery's end but with as little turmoil as possible and within constitutional boundaries and the framework of federalism.[1]

By November 1861 Lincoln had drafted two proposed bills for the state of Delaware, which he viewed as an ideal experimental ground in that it had fewer than eighteen hundred slaves as of the 1860 census. Under one proposal, Delaware would abolish slavery as of January 1, 1867; in the other, by January 1, 1893. Both versions had the federal government providing Delaware with U.S. bonds, with the implication that the state could compensate its slave owners as it saw fit. Moreover, Delaware could "make provision of apprenticeship," not to extend beyond the age of twenty-one for males or eighteen for females for all minors whose mothers were not free at the time of their birth. Neither bill was ever introduced.[2]

On March 6, 1862, Lincoln urged Congress that the federal government "ought to co-operate with any state which may adopt gradual abolishment of slavery" by "giving to such state pecuniary aid, to be used by such state in it's [*sic*] discretion, to compensate for the inconveniences public and private, produced by such change of system." Lincoln advised in his message, "In my judgment, gradual, and not sudden emancipation, is better for all," and he made a pragmatic argument by noting that the cost of the war would soon exceed the cost of purchasing the slaves in the states. Lincoln also assured that his proposed resolution created "no claim of a right, by federal authority, to interfere with slavery within state limits, referring, as it does, the absolute control of the subject, in each case, to the state and it's [*sic*] people, immediately interested."[3]

Many abolitionists voiced opposition to Lincoln's proposal, especially at the idea of gradual, not immediate, emancipation, though black spokesperson Frederick Douglass expressed hope at the thought of a president advocating emancipation in the first place. Slaveholders in the Border States lacked enthusiasm, too. On March 9, Lincoln met with Representative Francis P. Blair Jr. of Missouri, noting in disappointment that Border State members of Congress continued to call on him but remained silent about his proposal. Blair agreed to round up a delegation of Border State congressmen, who met with Lincoln the next day.[4]

Debate proved divisive when Congress took up the measure. Opponents called the measure unconstitutional as well as unfair in that free states would bear a financial cost due to slavery. In a letter to Democratic senator James A. McDougall of California, Lincoln made the point that "less than eighty seven days cost of this war would [at four hundred dollars per slave] pay for all in Delaware, Maryland, District of Columbia, Kentucky, and Missouri." Unswayed, McDougall delivered a speech challenging the constitutionality of using federal money for these purposes. In the end, though, Congress approved, and Lincoln signed on April 10, 1862, a joint resolution that tracked the language of Lincoln's proposal the previous month.[5]

Lincoln on April 16 also signed legislation immediately ending slavery in the District of Columbia. The act afforded loyal slave owners ninety days in which to request compensation and appropriated $100,000 to assist in colonization efforts for freedpeople who "may desire to emigrate," so long as the expenditure did not exceed a hundred dollars per person. An even bigger victory for Lincoln came on June 19, 1862, when he signed legislation immediately ending slavery in all U.S. territories and prohibiting it in any territories acquired in the future. Strikingly, the legislation ignored Taney's *Dred Scott* ruling that Congress could not regulate slavery in the territories. Moreover, the act did not provide for compensation, indicating diminishing concern with Taney's argument in his *Dred Scott* opinion regarding due process protection for property in human beings.[6]

Alongside these two victories, however, Lincoln's hope that the Border States would take up gradual compensated emancipation sputtered. On July 12, 1862, Lincoln impressed upon a congressional delegation from the Border States meeting with him at the White House that emancipation in the Border States would crush the rebellion because it would show the Confederate states that no other state would join them. Besides, Lincoln observed, if the war continued, slavery would be "extinguished by mere friction and abrasion—by the mere incidents of the war." Would it not be better for their constituents to secure "substantial compensation for that which is sure to be wholly lost" and, in the process, do something that would shorten the war? Lincoln assured the delegation that he did "not speak of emancipation *at once*, but of a *decision* at once to emancipate *gradually*." Land in South America could be cheaply purchased, Lincoln added, and "when numbers shall be large enough to be company and encouragement for one another, the freed people will not be so reluctant to go."[7]

The next day, while the Border State congressmen considered his statements, Lincoln traveled in a carriage along with Seward and Secretary of the Navy Gideon Welles to the funeral of Secretary of War Edwin M. Stanton's son. During this trip, Lincoln privately told Seward and Welles that he planned a separate initiative to address slavery in the states in rebellion: an emancipation proclamation. According to Lincoln, the matter had become a military necessity because the Confederacy relied on slaves to work on farms and fortifications, freeing up white men for military service.[8]

By July 14, 1862, twenty members of the Border States delegation signed a letter rejecting Lincoln's plan for their states. Seven other members of the delegation signed a document the next day indicating they would at least ask their constituents to consider Lincoln's recommendations. The majority response challenged the "constitutional power of this government to make appropriations of money for the object designated" and doubted the federal government even had the resources to pay such a sum. Seven of the twenty still served in Congress as of January 31, 1865, and three of them—Representatives Francis Thomas and Edwin H. Webster of Maryland and James S. Rollins of Missouri—voted in favor of the Thirteenth Amendment (the other four voted no).[9]

On that same day, July 14, Lincoln sent a draft bill to Congress that would appropriate compensation in the form of federal bonds to every state that ended slavery. The select committee on emancipation in the House reported a bill, but Congress adjourned before taking any further action on it. In fact, no state adopted subsidized emancipation.[10]

Circumstances on the military front influenced Lincoln's timing on announcing his intention to issue an emancipation proclamation. By the summer of 1862, military victories in the western theater functionally secured Missouri and Kentucky to the Union, and Maryland and Delaware seemed out of danger of trying to secede as well. Even if these states were not ready to consider emancipation themselves, the overall situation freed Lincoln to think about enacting emancipation on a broader scale, and without compensation, in the states in rebellion. Major General George B. McClellan's failure to capture the Confederate capital and his repulse in the Seven Days Battles near Richmond (June 25–July 1, 1862), moreover, stalled the Union war effort in the East. Something had to be done to intensify the pressure on the Confederacy, as slavery allowed it to mobilize white men into the armed forces. In this context, Lincoln on July 22, 1862, read to his cabinet a draft proclamation by which he would free the Confederacy's slaves in his capacity as commander-in-chief of the U.S. armed forces. Seward cautioned Lincoln to announce this decision after the Union had achieved a military victory, lest it appear to Europe as a desperate act.[11]

Lincoln seized the opportunity when McClellan repulsed General Robert E. Lee's invasion of Maryland. On September 22, 1862, Lincoln announced that as of January 1, 1863, all slaves within any state or part of a state in rebellion at that time would "be then, thenceforward, and forever free." Lincoln also stated that, when Congress reconvened, he would again recommend it provide financial aid for any states not in rebellion that wished to "voluntarily adopt" immediate or gradual abolition within their limits as well as continue efforts to "colonize persons of African descent, with their consent." Lincoln gave Confederate states a hundred-day period in which they could rejoin the Union and, if Congress went along, accept compensated emancipation. No Confederate state took Lincoln up on the offer.[12]

In the middle of this hundred-day period, Lincoln did something confusing: he spent about 40 percent of his Annual Message dated December 1, 1862, urging Congress to propose a package of constitutional amendments designed to induce individual states to pursue gradual emancipation. While impractical, poorly timed, and politically inexpedient, the package shows Lincoln's newfound willingness to use constitutional amendment to effect abolition alongside his continuing fidelity to federalism and commitment to state-based models.

Lincoln's first proposed amendment, marked by uncharacteristically complex wording, would grant federal compensation to every slave state to abolish bondage before 1900 in the form of interest-bearing U.S. bonds delivered in installments or at once, depending on whether abolition was gradual or immediate. Any state that afterward reintroduced or tolerated slavery would have to refund the value of the bonds received and all interest paid. Lincoln's second proposed amendment held more simply, "All slaves who shall have enjoyed actual freedom by the chances of the war, at any time before the end of the rebellion, shall be forever free; but all owners of such, who shall not have been disloyal, shall be compensated for them, at the same rates as is provided for States adopting abolishment of slavery, but in such way, that no slave shall be twice accounted for." Finally, Lincoln asked Congress to propose an amendment authorizing it to "appropriate money, and otherwise provide, for colonizing free colored persons, with their own consent, at any place or places without the United States."[13]

Lincoln explained that "without slavery the rebellion could never have existed; without slavery it could not continue." Lincoln admitted that different opinions existed as to what should be done with slavery—whether it should be allowed to continue, abolished immediately without compensation, or ended gradually with compensation—as well as about whether freedpeople ought to be colonized abroad or allowed to remain in the United States. He then warned against the waste of energy taking place "in struggles among ourselves," urging, "By mutual concession we should harmonize, and act together." Lincoln cast his proposal as "compromise among the friends, and not with the enemies of the Union."[14]

Lincoln then tried to counter a variety of anticipated criticisms of his plan, sometimes using unsatisfying or incomplete logic. For instance, Lincoln argued that the thirty-seven-year time frame in the first proposed amendment would spare the staunchest defenders of slavery from being upset by the measure because they likely would have died before 1900. Lincoln ignored the fact that, under his plan, some states might abolish slavery immediately. To critics who felt gradual emancipation gave "too little to the now living slaves," Lincoln answered, "It really gives them much," saving them "from the vagrant destitution which must largely attend immediate emancipation in localities where their numbers are very great" and giving "the inspiring assurance that their posterity shall be free forever"—not the same thing as immediate freedom from bondage.[15]

Lincoln also argued that his plan left federalism unaltered because it allowed each slave state to decide the pace of abolition on its own and without mandating that any two states proceed alike. Lincoln did not mention that accordingly, his proposal did not require nationwide abolition by a certain date. Under his plan, states could have chosen to reject federal compensation assistance and continued slavery into the twentieth century.[16]

Lincoln sought to assuage slaveholders by pointing out that they would receive compensation for what was "in a certain sense . . . the destruction of property." In words foreshadowing his Second Inaugural, Lincoln addressed the objections of those who were to pay and not receive: "The people of the south are not more responsible for the original introduction of this property, than are the people of the north; and when it is remembered how unhesitatingly we all use cotton and sugar, and share the profits of dealing in them, it may not be quite safe to say, that the south has been more responsible than the north for its continuance. If then, for a common object, this property is to be sacrificed is it not just that it be done at a common charge?"[17]

Finally, Lincoln argued, his emancipation scheme made practical sense: "If, with less money, or money more easily paid, we can preserve the benefits of the Union by this means, than we can by the war alone, is it not also economical to do it?" The war required large sums immediately, Lincoln continued, but compensated emancipation "would require no ready cash; nor the bonds even, any faster than the emancipation progresses." Moreover, Lincoln anticipated that it would likely take the full thirty-seven years to complete his plan, and at that time, the United States would "probably have a hundred millions of people to share the burden, instead of thirty one millions, as now." After offering a lengthy detour into demography, in which Lincoln explained how he came to this number (erroneously, as it turns out, for he overestimated the U.S. population in 1900 by about twenty-four million people), he regained the fundamental logic of his earlier argument: "the great advantage of a policy by which we shall not have to pay until we number a hundred millions, what, by a different policy, we would have to pay now, when we number but thirty one millions," and in a way that "will cost no blood, no precious life. It will be a saving of both."[18]

Lincoln briefly touched on his proposed second amendment, stating, "It would be impracticable to return to bondage the class of persons therein contemplated," and that because some of them, "in the property sense, belong to loyal owners . . . provision is made in this article for compensating such." The president then turned to his third proposed amendment as it related "to the future of the freed people," observing that it "does not oblige, but merely authorizes, Congress to aid in colonizing such as may consent." While stating, "I strongly favor colonization," Lincoln also addressed "an objection urged against free colored persons remaining in the country, which is largely imaginary, if not sometimes malicious": that the presence of freedpeople "would injure, and displace white labor and white laborers." As to arguments that "the freed people will swarm forth, and cover the whole land," Lincoln reminded that black people were "already in the land" and liberation would not make them any more numerous. Lincoln asked, "Why should emancipation south, send the free people north?" Lincoln then offered his answer: "People, of any color, seldom run, unless there be something to run from. *Heretofore* colored people, to some extent, have fled north from bondage; and *now*, perhaps, from both bondage and destitution. But if gradual emancipation and deportation be adopted, they will have neither to flee from. Their old masters will give them wages at least until new laborers can be procured; and the freed men, in turn, will gladly give their labor for the wages, till new homes can be found for them, in congenial climes, and with people of their own blood and race."[19]

Lincoln reminded those reading his proposal that he did not view adoption of his plan as a prerequisite for restoration of the Union, and he urged Congress while it was under consideration to pass other legislation to compensate states that may adopt emancipation. Moreover, the president assured, while Congress and the American people considered his plan, he would stay neither prosecution of the war nor the terms of his proclamation of September 22, 1862. "Its timely *adoption*," Lincoln added about his proposal, "would bring restoration and thereby stay both."[20]

The president also outlined the mechanics of amending the Constitution in a way that would guide his policy for ratifying the Thirteenth Amendment. In keeping with his position that the Confederate states had never left the Union, Lincoln stated: "The requisite three-fourths of the States will necessarily include seven of the Slave states. Their concurrence, if obtained, will give assurance of their severally adopting emancipation, at no very distant day, upon the new constitutional terms. This assurance would end the struggle now, and save the Union forever." Thus, Lincoln urged, his plan would "secure peace more speedily, and maintain it more permanently, than can be done by force alone," and with less cost, in blood and treasure, than war.[21]

Lincoln acknowledged the novelty of his plan, admitting, "The dogmas of the quiet past, are inadequate to the stormy present. . . . As our case is new, so we must think anew, and act anew." Lincoln saw his plan, embodied in a package of constitutional amendments, as the best way to save the Union and republican values worldwide: "We know how to save the Union. The world knows we do know how to save it. . . . In *giving* freedom to the *slave*, we *assure* freedom to the *free*—honorable alike in what we give, and what we preserve. We shall nobly save, or meanly lose, the last best, hope of earth. Other means may succeed; this could not fail. The way is plain, peaceful, generous, just—a way which, if followed, the world will forever applaud, and God must forever bless."[22]

Few people embraced Lincoln's plan. A few days before Lincoln transmitted the message, Secretary of the Treasury Salmon P. Chase asked the president to reconsider. "You did not ask my opinion of the particular plan developed, and, perhaps, I ought not to give it unasked," Chase began his letter. "Still I feel myself warranted by the very respect & affection I feel for you & my deep anxiety for the future of our country, in begging you to reflect whether . . . it would not be wise to forbear the introduction of the amendment of the Constitution." While Republicans might agree with Lincoln in general as to "the ends to be reached by the proclamation & compensated emancipation," Chase cautioned, "many of them will probably be averse to attempting any such amendments of the Constitution as you have embodied in your draft." Moreover, according to Chase, "no probability" existed that "any amendment of the constitution touching slavery" could command a vote of two-thirds of the Congress or the states (Chase here erred: three-fourths of the states need to ratify an amendment for it to take effect). Chase asked Lincoln, "Is it expedient to propose the measure if there is not a strong probability of its adoption? Will not such an act weaken rather than strengthen yourself and your administration?"[23]

Horace Greeley and African Americans reading with dismay Lincoln's gradual emancipation scheme as outlined in his 1862 Annual Message. "The Great Negro Emancipation" in *Harper's Weekly*, December 20, 1862. Courtesy of the American Antiquarian Society.

Polish count Adam Gurowski, serving as a translator in the State Department, described Lincoln's Annual Message as "uneasy, forced, tortuous," while Frederick Douglass felt that "the President is not competent to write his own official papers." Republican representative Henry L. Dawes of Massachusetts criticized the message on policy grounds, writing his wife, "How it makes one's heart bleed for his country to have its chief magistrate proposing measures to be accomplished in 1900 as a remedy for evils and perils which have thrust us . . . into the very jaws of death." Dawes added that while the survival of the Republic held in the balance, "The chief magistrate answers I've got a plan which is going to work well in the next century." On the other hand, at least some newspapers praised the plan: the *New York Times* called it "concise, clear and perspicuous," while the *Boston Journal* saw Lincoln's policy as "co-operative" with the Emancipation Proclamation, with that measure dealing with slavery in parts then in rebellion and Lincoln's new plan making emancipation universal, "so that the nineteenth century should close on no American slave."[24]

On December 11, 1862, during consideration by the House of Representatives of Lincoln's Annual Message, Republican representative John Hutchins of Ohio called Lincoln's plan "entirely impracticable" and unlikely to persuade the Confederates to end the war. According to Hutchins, the Emancipation Proclamation and successful prosecution of the war would "restore freedom to a race" and "secure peace to a continent." A few days later, Representative George Yeaman of Kentucky criticized emancipation in general and further argued that the "schemes of the proclamation and the message are alike impractical." Moreover, Yeaman maintained, the country would not bear the gigantic cost of compensating loyal owners as well as purchasing land and providing transport and at least some level of initial support for settlers in any colonization scheme. While the House referred Lincoln's plan to a special committee formed the previous session to deal with emancipation, the Senate did not even do that. Ultimately, no one in Congress proposed Lincoln's amendments.[25]

Two decades later, Representative James G. Blaine of Maine recalled that "Congress had scarcely time to consider" Lincoln's proposal before he issued the Emancipation Proclamation but that "Republican members of both branches" took up the matter "promptly and cordially." Blaine called the opposition of Border State legislators a "mistake," which cost their constituents a lot of money. Over four decades later, Cornelius Cole, who took office as representative from California on March 4, 1863, recollected more accurately that Lincoln's amendment proposal "recognized the ownership of the master to his slave," and because "many members of Congress could not agree with him in this," it "received no consideration by Congress."[26]

The timing of Lincoln's proposal also seems intellectually inconsistent, in that he followed his willingness to turn to the amendment process in late 1862 with hesitance and caution until mid-1864. Moreover, as Hutchins noted in his speech, the Constitution needed no amendment for Congress to have authority to appropriate money to help state emancipation or colonization schemes. This objection had been raised by several members of Congress, though, and Lincoln likely wanted to allay all fears on the point. Doing so in this way reflected a marked break from Lincoln's reaction when President Polk had proposed amending the Constitution if the people wanted the federal government to have the authority to make appropriations for internal improvements.[27]

Lincoln's proposal, coming exactly a month before his announced date for signing the Emancipation Proclamation, also confused the American people by creating doubt as to whether he really intended to do so. Lincoln had, in the words of historian Mark E. Neely Jr., temporarily lost his "political equilibrium." Perhaps Lincoln felt desperate to make one final attempt at inducing the Confederate states to put down their arms before he issued his Emancipation Proclamation. The plan was ill conceived, however—it is difficult to imagine that the amendments would be passed by Congress and sent to the states for ratification prior to January 1, 1863. The fact that Congress's response to Lincoln's plan matched Chase's prediction indicates that the president did not consult with its members to see how it would be received. And, even if Congress did somehow pass Lincoln's amendment package in time, what then? It could not be ratified in time, especially when Lincoln insisted on the inclusion of the Confederate states in the process.[28]

Thus, on January 1, 1863, Lincoln signed the Emancipation Proclamation in his capacity as "Commander-in-Chief, of the Army and Navy of the United States in time of actual armed rebellion against authority and government of the United States, and as a fit and necessary war measure for suppressing said rebellion." Lincoln specified areas he considered to be in rebellion, and thus within reach of the Emancipation Proclamation, and then declared the slaves within those areas to be "free," further announcing that the federal armed forces would not only "recognize and maintain the freedom of said persons" but recruit from among them as well. William Lloyd Garrison called the proclamation "sublime in its magnitude." Some Democrats excoriated it as unconstitutional and called it the death knell of the Union, believing it would sap army morale because white men would not fight or enlist for the cause of emancipation, while at the same time it would steel the Confederates to fight even harder. Other Democrats accepted the proclamation as an effective war measure designed to make the Confederacy weaker even while they remained unenthusiastic about freeing slaves.[29]

Lincoln cast the Emancipation Proclamation as a wartime measure within presidential war powers for a dual purpose: doing so not only grounded Lincoln's action on solid constitutional bedrock but also garnered the support of War Democrats. On the other hand, constitutional limits meant that slavery remained in the Border States and some areas of the Confederacy then under Union control that he exempted (portions of Louisiana and Virginia). Nonetheless, the Emancipation Proclamation had a real impact: it expanded the Union's war aims to include the end of slavery alongside reunification, and it afforded freedom to Confederate slaves as soon as they reached Union army lines. Many of them took action to make this happen. Politically, while the Democrats gained some representatives in the 1862 elections because of war weariness and opposition to Lincoln's suspension of habeas corpus and other policies, Republicans maintained control in the House and expanded their plurality in the Senate.

Almost immediately, people criticized the Emancipation Proclamation as unconstitutional. Benjamin R. Curtis, who had resigned from his seat on the Supreme Court not long after his dissent in the

Dred Scott case, published in 1862 a pamphlet titled *Executive Power* in which he criticized Lincoln's expansive view of his authority by citing the president's preliminary Emancipation Proclamation and habeas corpus policies. More recently, law professor Sanford Levinson has questioned the constitutionality of the proclamation but identifies the matter as irrelevant insofar as the moral value of ending slavery trumped strict constitutional construction. Another criticism comes from historian Richard Hofstadter, who claims the Emancipation Proclamation's bland language—the document had all the "moral grandeur of a bill of lading," Hofstadter observes—revealed Lincoln's tepid enthusiasm for emancipation.[30]

In reality, Lincoln faced political constraints that limited his ability to act, and his fidelity to working within the Constitution created further boundaries on the means at his disposal. Moreover, Lincoln drafted the Emancipation Proclamation as a legal document crafted to pass constitutional muster as a war measure. Legal historian Paul Finkelman astutely calls Lincoln's emancipation strategy "constitutionally innovative," which is different from unconstitutional. Moreover, in direct challenge to Levinson's contention, law professor Michael Stokes Paulsen observes that while emergency conditions do not expand constitutional power, they may allow for the exercise of constitutional powers that do not trigger until those conditions exist.[31]

The Emancipation Proclamation had a critical and direct impact on the Thirteenth Amendment. It further placed the ultimate fate of slavery into the center of constitutional and wartime discussion. Moreover, while the preliminary proclamation referenced the idea of compensated emancipation, the document Lincoln issued on January 1 did not, reflecting that he had abandoned concern with Fifth Amendment due process or takings clause arguments. Lincoln saw the usefulness of offering compensation to induce emancipation but no longer viewed doing so as necessary. Additionally, with the Emancipation Proclamation, Lincoln now used the federal government to address slavery in the states where it existed, in direct contrast to the position he took in his First Inaugural Address. While Lincoln still held that the Confederate states had never left the Union, he used the state of rebellion in them to declare free millions of slaves in states, not territories. Lincoln now ordered the executive department of the federal government, including the armed forces, to "recognize and maintain the freedom of said persons," and his Emancipation Proclamation allowed for black soldiers to join the Union army. This shift opened the door for the Thirteenth Amendment, which broadly projected federal power into a matter formerly left to the states' control. At the same time, the Emancipation Proclamation indicated Lincoln's desire to work within the Constitution, and he believed that he did so.[32]

While ill conceived, the amendments Lincoln proposed in December 1862 also revealed his willingness to change the Constitution, using the means provided in that document to eradicate slavery. At the same time, Lincoln's proposal affirmed his continued hope in the viability of state-based emancipation. While state-level action ultimately failed to provide a national resolution about slavery, Lincoln's work to foster dialogue about such programs did influence the course of the Thirteenth Amendment: discussion in states such as Maryland and Missouri about amending their constitutions to end slavery helped make more favorable the climate for proposing a national amendment to make the United States fully free.

C H A P T E R F O U R

THE ROAD TO AN ABOLITION AMENDMENT

After signing the Emancipation Proclamation, Lincoln made few public pronouncements about slavery until his August 1863 letter to James C. Conkling. In it, Lincoln professed, "I certainly wish that all men could be free," but claimed he had never proposed any measure that could be viewed as inconsistent with being for the Union. "I suggested compensated emancipation," Lincoln noted, to which people objected in that they did not wish to be taxed to "buy negroes." "But I had not asked you to be taxed to buy negroes," Lincoln added, "except in such way, as to save you from greater taxation to save the Union exclusively by other means." Lincoln also affirmed his deference to the will of the people, stating, "I freely acknowledge myself the servant of the people, according to the bond of service—the United States constitution; and that, as such, I am responsible to them." Lincoln then defended his Emancipation Proclamation on constitutional and practical grounds, but he used the image of black soldiers to reinforce his earlier statement that he wished all men could be free and to send a subtle message as to his end goal: "If they stake their lives for us, they must be prompted by the strongest motive—even the promise of freedom. And the promise being made, must be kept."[1]

At Gettysburg a few months later, Lincoln abstractly announced, "This nation, under God, shall have a new birth of freedom," but without making any direct reference to slavery. In neither the Conkling letter nor the Gettysburg Address did Lincoln reference specifics as to how to accomplish permanent nationwide freedom.[2]

In fact, Radical Republicans, anticipating the Confederacy's defeat, offered ways to address the problem without amending the Constitution. Solicitor of the War Department William Whiting proposed legislation requiring Confederate states to renounce slavery as a prerequisite to rejoining the Union, while Representative Henry Winter Davis of Maryland contended that the Constitution's Article IV, Section 4 Guarantee Clause ("The United States shall guarantee to every State in this Union a Republican Form of Government") allowed Congress to insist that Confederate state governments abolish slavery. Senator Charles Sumner of Massachusetts argued in an essay originally published in the *Atlantic Monthly* in October 1863 that by seceding, the Confederate states had committed suicide and thus could be treated as territories. According to Sumner, "The whole Rebel region . . . lapses under the exclusive jurisdiction of Congress, precisely as any other territory," and became "'a clean slate,' where Congress, under the Constitution of the United States, may write the laws." In addition to relying on the Constitution's Territory Clause, Sumner affirmed the Radical Republican argument that the Guarantee Clause also applied: "Whatever shows itself dangerous to a republican form of government must be removed without delay or hesitation."[3]

All these plans left the Constitution unchanged, could not address slavery in the Border States (though Radicals could argue that the Guarantee Clause would allow Congress to act in these states), and focused on the primacy of Congress over the state governments or president. As Sumner stated in his essay, "There are yet other words of the Constitution which cannot be forgotten: 'New States may be admitted by the Congress into this Union.' Assuming that the Rebel States are no longer *de facto* States of this Union, but that the territory occupied by them is within the jurisdiction of Congress, then these words become completely applicable. It will be for Congress, in such way as it shall think best, to regulate the return of these States to the Union, whether in time or manner."[4]

More conservative Republicans shuddered at the implications of Sumner's position for federalism. In an October 1863 speech,

Postmaster General Montgomery Blair warned that the senator's theory meant the "sheer abolition of State constitutions in the regions suffering under the rod of the rebellion," with Congress assuming "absolute power over the States recovered to the Union." Blair called such a doctrine "abhorrent to every principle on which the Union was founded." Blair preferred Lincoln's method: "He saves the State by putting the powers of the Government, as soon as they are redeemed, into the hands of loyal men; and then the State resumes its place in the councils of the nation with all its attributes and rights." While both groups of Republicans may have wanted slavery's demise, the Radicals wanted to compel abolition whereas moderates still sought to encourage Southern whites to emancipate through state constitutions.[5]

Thus, in August 1863, Lincoln wrote his commander of the Department of the Gulf, Major General Nathaniel P. Banks, concerning Louisiana: "While I very well know what I would be glad for Louisiana to do, it is quite a different thing for me to assume direction of the matter. I would be glad for her to make a new Constitution recognizing the emancipation proclamation, and adopting emancipation in those parts of the state to which the proclamation does not apply. And while she is at it, I think it would not be objectionable for her to adopt some practical system by which the two races could gradually live themselves out of their old relation to each other, and both come out better prepared for the new. Education for young blacks should be included in the plan." The following month, Lincoln wrote his military governor of Tennessee, Andrew Johnson, urging that the time had come to inaugurate a loyal state government there. Lincoln added, "I see that you have declared in favor of emancipation in Tennessee, for which, may God bless you. Get emancipation into your new State government—Constitution—and there will be no such word as fail for your case." Blair cited Lincoln's policy toward both states in his October 1863 speech.[6]

In early September 1863, Lincoln also wrote Salmon P. Chase concerning his secretary of the Treasury's "great anxiety," in Lincoln's words, in urging that the Emancipation Proclamation should "now be applied" to the parts of Virginia and Louisiana previously exempted from it. Lincoln explained to Chase that the proclamation's only constitutional justification came as a "military measure" and therefore "did not apply to the exempted localities." Moreover, Lincoln noted, it still did not apply, and he asked, "If I take the step must I not do so, without the argument of military necessity, and so, without any argument, except the one that I think the measure politically expedient, and morally right?" Lincoln emphasized his concerns with a series of questions: "Would I not thus give up all footing upon constitution or law? Would I not thus be in the boundless field of absolutism? Could this pass unnoticed, or unresisted? Could it fail to be perceived that without any further stretch, I might do the same in Delaware, Maryland, Kentucky, Tennessee, and Missouri; and even change any law in any state? Would not many of our own friends shrink away appalled? Would it not lose us the elections, and with them, the very cause we seek to advance?"[7]

At the end of September, Lincoln reiterated the point during a meeting with a delegation of Radicals from Missouri and Kansas, to whom he explained, "The mode of emancipation in Missouri is not my business. That is a matter which belongs exclusively to the citizens of that state: I do not wish to interfere." Lincoln provided some advice, though: "I desire, if it pleases the people of Missouri, that they should adopt gradual emancipation. I think that your division upon this subject jeopardizes the grand result. I think that a union of all anti-slavery men upon this point would have made emancipation a final fact forever."[8]

While Lincoln continued to urge state-based gradual emancipation schemes, at least for slaveholding states within the Union, some of his advisors discussed a different approach: amending the Constitution. In a meeting with Leonard Swett in October 1863, Lincoln's friend raised growing criticism by the Radical Republicans that the president remained too conservative. Swett told Lincoln that the time had arrived when Congress would pass a resolution for an amendment abolishing slavery and that, in taking the lead on the measure, Lincoln could put himself in advance of the Radicals: "No one could maintain himself upon any measure more radical, and if [Lincoln] failed to take the position, his rivals would." Yet Lincoln would have none of it at this time, and he instead asked Swett, "Is not that question [of emancipation] doing well enough now?" When Swett answered that it was, Lincoln replied, "I have never done an official act with a view to promote my own personal aggrandizement, and I don't like to begin now, I can see that time coming; whoever can wait for it will see it—whoever stands in its way, will be run over by it."[9]

In early December 1863, Representative Isaac N. Arnold of Illinois wrote Lincoln a confidential letter giving advice regarding the president's upcoming Annual Message to Congress. "You have given the institution the hardest blows it has ever received," stated Arnold, continuing, "Complete the work you have begun. End slavery during your administration." Toward that end, Arnold advised Lincoln to do three things in his Annual Message: reiterate his desire that the Border States abolish slavery on their own as well as his willingness to see the federal government aid them in their endeavor; recommend Congress pass legislation to make permanent the freedom of all slaves in all the territory embraced by the Emancipation Proclamation and thus eliminate any question as to whether wartime freedom for these slaves would revert to peacetime slavery; and recommend "a change in the Constitution so as to prohibit slavery in every part of the United States." Arnold echoed Swett's advice by suggesting to Lincoln that following this plan would prevent any split among the Republican Party for the upcoming presidential election and guarantee that his "nomination and election will be almost a matter of course."[10]

Moreover, by autumn 1863, increasing numbers of War Democrats were calling for slavery's end, some of them motivated by the military benefits of emancipation, others recognizing moral arguments, and still others appreciating the political liability of defending a dying institution. In Ohio, John Brough, who would take office in January 1864 as that state's governor, proclaimed, "Slavery must be wiped out and the slaves once free must not be re-enslaved." In Arkansas, Edward L. Gantt recognized the threat posed to state and local authority by Radical Republican proposals and thus recommended abolition of slavery so as to preserve federalism: "By thus *formally giving up* what is *already lost*, we will have secured to us, all our rights as equal States in the Union." A convention of the Northwestern

War Democrats held in Chicago in November 1863, declared, "We shall not regret if slavery falls as the legitimate consequence of the war," and one of its delegates, James W. Taylor of Minnesota, had even written Salmon P. Chase to propose a coalition of antislavery Democrats and Republicans under the slogan "A *Union as it was and the constitution as it is* (or as *it may be amended*)."[11]

Even some prominent Irish Americans, generally loyal to the Democratic Party, moved on the issue. In a speech in 1861, Thomas F. Meagher stated, "There is not a single proposition of the Republican party to which I say 'Yea.'" Yet by fall 1863, the former commander of the Irish Brigade described slavery as a "cancerous disease, as it was the glaring disgrace, of this great nation, and a violent contradiction of the principles on which it was established." Lincoln had made similar arguments and analogies in the 1850s. Meagher claimed he had earlier accepted slavery because it was part of the Union to which he was devoted, but "the rebellion of the South emancipated all true Republicans from their complicity with an ordained system of bondage."[12]

Despite the advice of Sweet and Arnold and discussion among some Democrats about the need to abolish slavery, Lincoln said nothing about amending the Constitution in his December 1863 Annual Message. Instead, the president highlighted state-based efforts toward emancipation, noting that in Tennessee and Arkansas, "owners of slaves and advocates of slavery at the beginning of the rebellion, now declare openly for emancipation in their respective States." Maryland and Missouri, Lincoln observed, "neither of which three years ago would tolerate any restraint upon the extension of slavery into new territories, only dispute now as to the best mode of removing it within their own limits." After affirming that he would "not attempt to retract or modify the emancipation proclamation; nor shall I return to slavery any person who is free by the terms of that proclamation, or by any of the acts of Congress," Lincoln declared he would nonetheless acquiesce "in any reasonable temporary State arrangement for the freed people . . . made with the view of possibly modifying the confusion and destitution which must, at best, attend all classes by a total revolution of labor throughout whole States. It is hoped that the already deeply afflicted people in those States may be somewhat more ready to give up the cause of their affliction, if, to this extent, this vital matter be left to themselves."[13]

This position contrasted with the advice of Salmon P. Chase, who a short while earlier had warned Lincoln, "My own strong impression is that special legislation for colored citizens will be as unnecessary as for white citizens. The demand for labor will secure them employment, and freedom will enable them to buy and build with the proceeds of their labor; while the voluntary charities, already so widely awakened, will, with proper countenance and support from the Government, secure to them the benefits of education and religion. Whether I am right or wrong in this, it seems to me clear that no, even apparent, sanction of legislation which may be easily perverted into virtual re-enslavement should be contained in the document you are about to put forth." Appointed to the Supreme Court by Lincoln, Chase would, in his capacity as a circuit judge, in 1867 strike down a Maryland apprenticeship program for black children as a violation of the Thirteenth Amendment.[14]

Toward the end of the message, Lincoln again recognized ongoing state-level efforts toward emancipation as "matters of profound gratulation" and affirmed that his "general views and feelings" on the topic "remain unchanged." Instead of offering any specific plan, as he had the previous year, Lincoln simply urged Congress to "omit no fair opportunity of aiding these important steps to a great consummation." Lincoln closed his message by identifying "the war power" as "still our main reliance" and by stating that to the armed forces "the world must stand indebted for the home of freedom disenthralled, regenerated, enlarged, and perpetuated."[15]

On the same day Lincoln sent to Congress his Annual Message, he issued a Proclamation of Amnesty and Reconstruction in which he offered a pardon to most Confederates if they took an oath to support the Constitution and all acts and proclamations made by Congress and the president concerning slavery. Lincoln then outlined a lenient Reconstruction proposal: in any Confederate state other than Virginia (where he and Congress recognized a loyal state government led by Governor Francis H. Pierpont), 10 percent of its 1860 voters could take the oath, "re-establish a State government which shall be republican," and amend the state constitution to abolish slavery, whereupon "such shall be recognized as the true government of the State."[16]

Consistent with his prior position that the states had not left the Union, Lincoln rejected Radical Republican theories and instead continued to seek emancipation through state constitutions. Also consistent with his Annual Message, Lincoln added in this proclamation that he would not oppose "any provision which may be adopted by such State government in relation to the freed people of such State, which shall recognize and declare their permanent freedom, provide for their education, and which may yet be consistent, as a temporary arrangement, with their present condition as a laboring, landless, and homeless class." Lincoln added the caveat that, "whether members sent to Congress from any State shall be admitted to seats, constitutionally rests exclusively with the respective Houses, and not to any extent with the Executive," and he left room for other proposals concerning emancipation and reconstruction.[17]

While Lincoln still looked to state-based emancipation, however, some members of Congress turned to constitutional amendment to address the matter. On December 14, 1863, Republican representative James M. Ashley of Ohio proposed to submit to the states a constitutional amendment prohibiting slavery or involuntary servitude in all states and territories then existing or to be acquired in the future. That same day, Republican representative James F. Wilson of Iowa proposed a similar amendment prohibiting slavery and involuntary servitude except as a punishment for crime and added a second paragraph authorizing Congress "to enforce the foregoing section of this article by appropriate legislation." Rather than arguing that the Guarantee Clause or some other provision of the Constitution applied, Ashley and Wilson proposed changing the Constitution to make it clear. After the holiday break, on January 11, 1864, Unionist senator John B. Henderson of Missouri proposed in that chamber a joint resolution for amending the Constitution to hold, "Slavery or involuntary servitude, except as a punishment for crime, shall not exist in the United States." Coming from a former slaveholder and Democrat, Henderson's statement sent a strong signal.[18]

Republican Representative Isaac N. Arnold of Illinois met with Lincoln on January 1, 1864, and recalled saying to him, "I hope Mr. President, one year from to-day I may have the pleasure of congratulating you on the consummation of three events which seem now very probable." When Lincoln asked what they were, Arnold replied, "First, That the rebellion may be completely crushed. Second, That slavery may be entirely destroyed, and prohibited forever throughout the Union. Third, That Abraham Lincoln may have been triumphantly reelected President of the United States." Lincoln replied "with a twinkle in his eye," according to Arnold, "I think I would compromise, by obtaining the first two propositions."[19]

As various members of Congress discussed amending the Constitution, Lincoln remained publicly silent. On February 7, 1864, a leader of the Republican Party in Indiana, John D. Defrees, advised Lincoln, "Why not send a message to Congress recommending the passage of a joint resolution proposing an amendment to the Constitution forever prohibiting slavery in the States and territories?" If Swett and Arnold expressed concern over the loyalty of Radical Republicans to the president, Defrees raised the possibility the Democrats would co-opt the issue. "It would be *your* measure," Defrees noted, and "if not done very soon the proposition *will* be presented by the Democracy and claimed by them as *their* proposition. This may look strange to those who do not remember with what *facility* that party can change front." Besides being "right in itself" and calculated to "have a beneficial influence on our election next fall," Defrees added, a constitutional amendment would eliminate one fear some people expressed concerning state-based emancipation, that a state could amend its constitution to prohibit slavery and then revert back a few years later. Finally, Defrees claimed, a "single amendment . . . would not open the whole constitution to amendment," and he noted that "if done, it would be in accordance with the mode provided by the constitution itself for its amendment—to which no one could reasonably object."[20]

Yet, Lincoln simply responded to Defrees the next day, "Our own friends have this under consideration now, and will do as much without a Message as with it." On the same day Lincoln wrote Defrees,

Senator Charles Sumner of Massachusetts proposed his own amendment to add the issue of equal rights into the discussion: "Everywhere within the limits of the United States, and of each State or Territory thereof, all persons are equal before the law, so that no person can hold another as a slave."[21]

A few days later, on February 10, 1864, a delegation of Protestant ministers presented to Lincoln a different type of amendment proposal. They wanted to reference God in the Constitution's preamble, linking that omission with the current war, and to include securing the rights of life, liberty, and the pursuit of happiness as one of the reasons for establishing the Constitution. Lincoln responded politely to the "general aspect" of the movement but added, "In regard to particulars, I must ask time to deliberate, as the work of amending the Constitution should not be done hastily," and he assured the ministers he would "carefully examine" their suggestion.[22]

Lincoln, in the first part of 1864, remained publicly quiet about amending the Constitution, and he continued to urge state-based emancipation. In January 1864, he ordered Major General Frederick Steele in Arkansas to work "with all possible vigor" with civilians there who proposed an election in that state that would include modifying the state constitution to eliminate slavery. To Republican representative John A. J. Creswell of Maryland, Lincoln in March confided privately that he felt "very anxious for emancipation to be effected in Maryland." As to the form, Lincoln stated that he thought gradual emancipation "would produce less confusion, and destitution, and therefore would be more satisfactory; but if those who are better acquainted with the subject, and are more deeply interested in it, prefer the *immediate*, most certainly I have no objection to their judgment prevailing," so long as everyone cooperated, for fear that "the friends of emancipation themselves may divide, and lose the measure altogether." A week and a half later, Lincoln sent Creswell another note: "It needs not to be a secret, that I wish success to emancipation in Maryland. It would aid much to end the rebellion. Hence it is a matter of national consequence." On February 9, Maryland's legislature enacted a bill calling for an election for delegates to a state constitutional convention to open on April 27, 1864.[23]

Between the summer of 1863 and the summer of 1864, Lincoln also began to think about what freedom for the slaves would look like. Lincoln had long talked about gradual emancipation, and he acknowledged that the transition from slavery to freedom would involve an adjustment for both white and black people. In his August 1863 letter to Major General Nathaniel P. Banks, Lincoln urged for Louisiana "some practical system by which the two races could gradually live themselves out of their old relation to each other," and he felt education should be part of the plan. In his Annual Message of 1863 and the Proclamation of Amnesty and Reconstruction, Lincoln reiterated the point.[24]

By early 1864, Lincoln also began to consider political rights for black people. On March 3, 1864, Arnold Bertonneau and Jean Baptiste Roudanez presented Lincoln with a petition signed by over a thousand free black men from Louisiana calling for their voting rights. During a cordial meeting, the president told the delegation that he could not impose such a condition on the states but would refer the matter to Louisiana's constitutional convention—another instance of Lincoln's respect for federalism. Lincoln remained true to his word—on March 13, he wrote to congratulate Michael Hahn on his election as governor and added, "Now you are about to have a Convention which, among other things, will probably define the elective franchise. I barely suggest for your private consideration, whether some of the colored people may not be let in—as, for instance, the very intelligent, and especially those who have fought gallantly in our ranks. They would probably help, in some trying time to come, to keep the jewel of liberty within the family of freedom. But this is only a suggestion, not to the public, but to you alone." Instead of talking about colonization, Lincoln now looked to an integrated multiracial society and endorsed the concept of enfranchising black men.[25]

While Lincoln remained publicly quiet about whether to amend the Constitution, some people argued that the time had not yet arrived for it. On February 11, 1864, the *New York Times* cautioned against the distraction of an amendment proposal during the upcoming presidential election, advising that focus had to remain on crushing the rebellion. In the opinion of the *Times*, "when the war is over and the Union restored, Congress can then, if it thinks proper, amend the Constitution in the way proposed." A few days later, the *Times* again warned against the "throwing of a new apple of discord into the arena!" While acknowledging that a constitutional amendment might be the ultimate solution for the slavery issue, the editorial pointed out that winning the war was the only way for abolitionism to triumph: "We say that not only true loyalty, but consistent Anti-Slavery itself, forbids this unseasonable introduction of a new political Anti-Slavery issue. It is absolutely certain that the anxiety of Northern abolitionists to kill Slavery can never be gratified unless this war against the rebellion succeeds. If the 'Confederacy' acquires its independence, Slavery there will be as secure from their hostility as Slavery in Cuba or in Brazil."[26]

In fact, the only Republican newspapers to support amending the Constitution at the time were those that were hostile to Lincoln. Some Republicans hesitated to support the measure, fearing that it would create an electoral backlash, especially if it forced the party to address the more controversial matter of rights for black people (see, for instance, Sumner's amendment proposal). Besides, the measure did not have the necessary two-thirds votes in the House anyway, so why get into a political morass? On the other hand, the Republican Party risked splintering, as the more radical wing contemplated replacing Lincoln with Salmon P. Chase until Chase issued a public letter that ended the movement.[27]

Thus, Lincoln remained quiet regarding the amendment while Congress discussed it. On March 19, 1864, Representatives Isaac N. Arnold of Illinois and James Wilson of Iowa delivered speeches in Congress that folded together Lincoln, Republican policy, and an antislavery amendment. Arnold told Republicans, "Our greatest danger arises from insane divisions among ourselves." In the next breath, Arnold named Lincoln, Lieutenant General Ulysses S. Grant, and Chase as "great leaders," and he called Lincoln the "Apostle of Liberty," assuring that when he left office in 1869, everyone would be "secured in the enjoyment of 'life, liberty, and the pursuit of happiness,'" and all men would stand "equal before the law." Wilson immediately followed Arnold in giving a lengthy speech in favor of an amendment. Republican organs treated the orations as campaign speeches, and historian Michael Vorenberg suggests that Lincoln may have asked Arnold and Wilson to speak on his behalf in an effort to unify Republicans. On the other hand, no correspondence between Lincoln and Arnold or Wilson survives in the matter, nor is there any reference to Lincoln meeting with either of them in person around this time. They may simply have been acting on their own to force the issue.[28]

A political shock came on April 5, 1864, when Democratic senator Reverdy Johnson of Maryland, in a speech in the Senate that the *New York Times* the next day called "remarkably brilliant," endorsed the amendment put forward by the Senate Judiciary Committee that combined the proposals by Ashley, Wilson, and Henderson (but rejected Sumner's language). That paper reported, "Union Senators crowded around him with hearty congratulations when he closed," while "Copperheads only scowled." The next day, Maryland's voters overwhelmingly approved holding a state constitutional convention. On April 7, Senator John B. Henderson of Missouri spoke in favor of the amendment. These speeches by two of Lincoln's friends went beyond partisanship to focus on the issue of slavery as the cause of the war. Henderson also noted the conservative nature of the amendment when compared to the plans of the Radical Republicans: "When the amendment has been adopted this doctrine of State suicide and territorial reorganization may be safely abandoned. The motive for such legislation is to be found in the great desire to which I have alluded—to get rid of slavery."[29]

Some opponents in the Senate, such as Garrett Davis of Kentucky, countered with a strained reading of Article V, claiming that amending the Constitution to abolish slavery went too far because the Founders had accepted the institution. Johnson and Henderson each responded to this argument by noting that because the Founders permitted slavery did not mean they precluded amending the Constitution to address it. Other senators argued the amendment inappropriately injected the federal government in a matter properly left for determination by the states. On April 8, 1864, the Senate voted 38 to 6 to approve a resolution that the Constitution should be amended to abolish slavery, with the only negative votes coming from the Delaware and Kentucky delegations and from Thomas A. Hendricks of Indiana and James A. McDougall of California. Five Border State senators and three free state Democrats voted in favor.[30]

Yet Lincoln continued to remain silent about the amendment. Finally, a short-lived fracture occurred in the Republican Party. A splinter group, the Radical Democracy, held a convention in Cleveland and adopted a platform on May 31, 1864, supporting suppression of the Confederacy, confiscation of rebel lands, vesting reconstruction in Congress and not in the Executive, and proposing constitutional amendments to prohibit slavery and "secure to all men absolute equality before the law," to limit presidents to one term, and to require their election "by a direct vote of the people." Just as Defrees had warned in February, some Democrats joined this short-lived movement, believing it would fragment the Republican Party. The movement nominated John C. Frémont, the Republican presidential nominee in 1856, for president, but he dropped out of the contest in September after the fall of Atlanta.[31]

At last, the time had come for Lincoln to endorse the idea of an abolition amendment. On one hand, it is tempting to see the platform of the Radical Democracy, the Frémont candidacy, and talk among Radical Republicans of replacing Lincoln as the party nominee as forcing Lincoln's hand. In reality, Lincoln probably wanted to allow public opinion on the issue to build (while he subtly helped to shape it) and to endorse an antislavery amendment when it became politically viable to do so and at a time when presidential support would have meaningful impact. After a tepid response to his state-based compensated emancipation schemes and questions swirling around his Emancipation Proclamation, Lincoln hesitated to churn the potentially divisive issue in 1863. Now, however, with some Border State senators declaring they favored an amendment abolishing slavery, when even some Democrats started to embrace the idea, and in anticipation that Grant's and Major General William T. Sherman's campaigns against Richmond and Atlanta would win the war, Lincoln's astute political sense told him the tipping point had arrived in mid-1864.

CHAPTER FIVE

REELECTION AND THE POLITICS OF CONSTITUTIONAL CHANGE

By June 1864 Lincoln had announced his support for amending the Constitution to make freedom national, suggesting to Senator Edwin D. Morgan of New York, who also served as chair of the Republican National Committee, that at its upcoming convention the party should include the measure as part of its platform. In 1895 reporter Noah Brooks recalled meeting with Lincoln shortly before the opening of the convention, and while Lincoln would not express an opinion as to the vice presidential candidate, he did "say that he hoped that the convention would declare in favor of the constitutional amendment abolishing slavery as one of the articles of the party faith."[1]

While avoiding a specific discussion of what such an amendment would mean or commenting on the amendment pending in Congress, the Republican National Convention took Lincoln's suggestion and adopted a plank calling for a constitutional amendment that "shall terminate and forever prohibit the existence of slavery within the limits or the jurisdiction of the United States." When a delegation from the convention met with Lincoln on June 9, 1864, he expressed his "gratitude" for his renomination and then spent most of his short address endorsing the amendment: "I approve the declaration in favor of so amending the Constitution as to prohibit slavery throughout the nation. When the people in revolt, with a hundred days of explicit notice, that they could, within those days, resume their allegiance, without the overthrow of their institution, and that they could not so resume it afterwards, elected to stand out, such [an] amendment of the Constitution as [is] now proposed, became a fitting, and necessary conclusion to the final success of the Union cause. Such alone can meet and cover all cavils. Now, the unconditional Union men, North and South, perceive its importance, and embrace it. In the joint names of Liberty and Union, let us labor to give it legal form, and practical effect." Theodore Tilton, editor of the *New York Independent*, reported in his paper on the meeting with the delegation: "When one of us mentioned the great enthusiasm at the Convention, after Senator E. D. Morgan's proposition to amend the Constitution, abolishing slavery, Mr. Lincoln instantly said, 'It was I who suggested to Mr. Morgan that he should put that idea into his opening speech.'" Lincoln knew his statement would be reprinted in newspapers. By taking credit for the proposal, he used the press to publicize his position on amending the Constitution to end slavery and to make it an issue in his 1864 reelection campaign.[2]

John Z. Goodrich, collector of the port of Boston and a delegate to the convention, wrote Lincoln excitedly within days to congratulate him on his endorsement of the amendment. Goodrich called Lincoln's action "very timely, & said in a way to show that it was a subject you had thoroughly considered long ago, & foresaw the necessity of such an amendment." Goodrich regarded the matter "as second in importance to no purpose than that has been presented to the country since the Government was founded," adding that "the enthusiasm & unanimity with which it was accepted by the Convention, composed of hunker Democrats, (formerly hunker) Whigs, Republicans, & radical free soilers, was all but an assurance that the people will adopt it, & that it will receive legal form & effect in the shortest possible time after the next election." Goodrich predicted, "The work of Ages (as it has commonly been regarded) will be accomplished during the Presidency of a single man."[3]

William Lloyd Garrison also cheered Lincoln's stance. Garrison wrote to the brother of John Cardinal Newman in July 1864 to acknowledge certain constitutional constraints on Lincoln's ability to act, adding that to many abolitionists, "Mr. Lincoln has seemed exceedingly slow in all his emancipatory measures. For this he has been severely chided, in the *Liberator* and out of it; and, for a time, a pro-slavery purpose was attributed to him, which I am now satisfied was not his animating spirit." According to Garrison, "It was only a proof of the great circumspection which controlled his acts with reference to the formidable rebellion at the South, and the fearfully divided state of public sentiment at the North, especially on the slavery question." After acknowledging that "the possibility of preserving the supremacy of the government and restoring the union of the States is still an open question," Garrison declared, "Yet what long strides he has taken in the right direction, and never a backward step! What grand and far-reaching anti-slavery measures have been consummated under his Administration! How near he has brought us—if the Government succeed in asserting its rightful supremacy over the rebellious States—to that glad day of jubilee."[4]

Garrison then traced how Lincoln brought abolitionism to the mainstream and helped to shape public opinion to pave the way for constitutional reform. At the time of Lincoln's inauguration, Garrison recounted, "the real abolition strength of the country [was] numerically insignificant, and politically speaking, of no importance—prejudice against the negro strong and universal—a general disposition, for a long period subsequently, to avoid the issue with slavery, and to endeavor to restore 'the Union as it was,' and even worse than it was, with all its pro-slavery compromises." According to Garrison, "This was all the moral and political capital Mr. Lincoln had to trade upon for the benefit of the despised and oppressed colored people; yet he has done a vast and truly magnificent business." The Emancipation Proclamation delivered a "virtual death blow to the whole slave system," Garrison reported, followed by the arming of tens of thousands of black men and other developments culminating in, "finally, the loyal sentiment of the country pledged to the amendment of the Constitution, forever prohibiting slavery in the land!"[5]

Despite the overwhelming vote in the Senate in April and Lincoln's endorsement in June, a highly partisan debate erupted in the House. On June 15, 1864, supporters of the amendment fell short by thirteen votes of the necessary two-thirds vote in favor by members in attendance.

All Republicans voted for the measure and all but four Democrats voted against it. The *New York Times*, which previously opposed the timing of the amendment, now voiced "regret" at its defeat and argued, "It imposes a needless delay upon the consummation of a great measure, without which the struggle between the South and the North can reach no end." The editorial now held, "The Union party then, has two momentous objects before it: the reelection of President LINCOLN, so as to insure that the war shall be prosecuted until the last rebel soldier lays down his arms, and the election of two-thirds of the members of the next Congress, so as to give the States authority to entertain the amendment abolishing all Slavery in the land forever."[6]

As a procedural matter, the manager for the resolution, Representative James M. Ashley, changed his vote from aye to nay so that he could call the House to reconsider the matter in the following session. Ashley pinned his hopes on the upcoming election, announcing his strategy on June 28, 1864: "When the verdict of the people is rendered next November, I trust this Congress will return determined to ingraft that verdict into the national Constitution." Both Ashley and the *Times* were right: everything now hinged on the election.[7]

Almost six months had lapsed between Ashley's initial amendment proposal and Lincoln's endorsement of it. One possibility for the delay was Lincoln's Whiggish deference to the legislature; he wanted Congress to debate the matter on its own. John C. Frémont's presidential candidacy and criticism from rival Republicans had pushed Lincoln to act, but he also relied on his political sense, preferring to remain silent and allow public support for the measure to build rather than to make any pronouncement that would inflame his opponents to charge him with prioritizing emancipation over the Union. Moreover, Lincoln continued to support state-based emancipation in places like Louisiana, Arkansas, Tennessee, Missouri, and Maryland, efforts that comported with his long-held agenda that slavery should be addressed by the states where it existed.

By June 1864, however, Lincoln saw that amending the Constitution to abolish slavery had a number of purposes beyond its moral implications. Lincoln wanted to use the amendment to unify the

Republicans, and even appeal to War Democrats, with a measure that could be read in various ways: it spoke of freedom but did not define what that meant and thus did not force the discussion of rights for the freedpeople. Moreover, as Generals Grant and Sherman started their campaigns toward Richmond and Atlanta, respectively, in May 1864, Lincoln believed he had finally found his winning team of generals. If correct, the progress of the federal armies would secure the Union militarily, allowing for greater popular support for an abolition amendment. Lincoln also wanted to put the matter of nationwide freedom out of his hands and into those of the people via the amendment process at a time when they would be receptive to it, so that it could not be an issue during any peace negotiations with the Confederates.

Additionally, Lincoln recognized what Senator Reverdy Johnson, Senator John B. Henderson, and Postmaster General Montgomery Blair had feared: Radical Republican theories threatened state identities and federalism. Lincoln's concern on this point is highlighted by his pocket veto of the Wade-Davis Bill in July 1864, a measure proposed by Senator Benjamin Wade of Ohio and Representative Henry Winter Davis of Maryland in response to what they felt was an overly lenient plan outlined by Lincoln in his Proclamation of Amnesty and Reconstruction. Not only would the Wade-Davis Bill derail Lincoln's efforts to build ties with Southern moderates, and his efforts to restore the state governments in Louisiana, Arkansas, and Tennessee, but it would have established Congress as the preeminent body in control of Reconstruction and truncated federalism by abolishing slavery in the states where it existed by legislation.

The Wade-Davis Bill would have required Lincoln to appoint provisional governors for the Confederate states, with the Senate's consent, and a majority of each state's white male citizens to take an oath to support the Constitution prior to the calling of a mandatory convention tasked with revising each state constitution. These new state constitutions had to include provisions disbarring certain civil and military officers from voting for or holding certain offices, abolishing slavery and guaranteeing the freedom of all persons in said state, and repudiating Confederate and state debts. After a majority of the people of the state entitled to vote under the bill had ratified the state constitution, the president, after obtaining Congress's assent, could recognize the state government. Then, the state could elect senators, representatives, and presidential electors. The bill also declared, "All persons held to involuntary servitude or labor in the states aforesaid are hereby emancipated and discharged therefrom, and they and their posterity shall be forever free."[8]

According to Lincoln's assistant John Hay, on July 4, 1864, Senator Zachariah Chandler of Michigan entered the ornate President's Room in the Capitol while Lincoln was signing bills on the last day of the congressional session. Chandler asked if he had signed the Wade-Davis Bill, to which Lincoln responded in the negative and offered, "This bill was placed before me a few minutes before Congress adjourns. It is a matter of too much importance to be swallowed in that way." After claiming that a veto would harm Republicans in Michigan and Ohio, Chandler stated that the "important point" of the bill was its provision prohibiting slavery in the reconstructed states. When Lincoln said, "That is the point on which I doubt the authority of Congress to act," Chandler responded, "It is no more than you have done yourself," and Lincoln ended the conversation by stating, "I conceive that I may in an emergency do things on military grounds which cannot be done constitutionally by Congress."[9]

Chandler departed and Lincoln continued speaking to other people in the room: "I do not see how any of us now can deny and contradict all we have always said, that congress has no constitutional power over slavery in the states. This bill and this position of these gentlemen seems to me to make the fatal admission (in asserting that the insurrectionary states are no longer states in the Union) that states whenever they please may of their own motion dissolve their connection with the Union. Now we cannot survive that admission I am convinced." Here, then, Lincoln announced another use for the proposed antislavery amendment: "It was to obviate this question that I earnestly favored the movement for an amendment to the Constitution abolishing slavery, which passed the Senate and failed in the House. I thought it much better, if it were possible, to restore the Union without the necessity of a violent quarrel among its friends, as to whether certain states have been in or out of the Union during the war: a merely metaphysical question and one unnecessary to be forced into discussion." According to Hay, Secretary of State William H. Seward, Secretary of the Interior John P. Usher, and Senator William Pitt Fessenden (who absented himself from the vote on the Wade-Davis Bill and thought it too radical a measure) agreed with Lincoln. Hay did not record the reaction of Senator Charles Sumner, also present in the room, though one can imagine his disapproval.[10]

A few days later, Lincoln explained his pocket veto even though he did not need to do so. Besides his unwillingness to be "inflexibly committed to any single plan of restoration," Lincoln felt "unprepared to declare, that the free-state constitutions and governments, already adopted and installed in Arkansas and Louisiana, shall be set aside and held for nought," claiming that doing so would have the effect of "repelling and discouraging the loyal citizens who have set up the same, as to further effort." Moreover, Lincoln did not wish to "declare a constitutional competency in Congress to abolish slavery in States," though he announced he was "at the same time sincerely hoping and expecting that a constitutional amendment, abolishing slavery throughout the nation, may be adopted."[11]

For Lincoln, eliminating the identity of the rebel states was out of the question, and he could not envision anything other than their restoration to normal relations within the Union with their full jurisdiction unharmed. Lincoln recognized that amending the Constitution would help to preserve federalism by precluding more radical proposals. As a practical matter, under his unwavering position that no state had left the Union, Lincoln knew that a number of Confederate states would need to approve any amendment so as to get it ratified. This fact provided Lincoln with another reason to oppose the Wade-Davis Bill and to move along the process of restoring the governments in states like Arkansas, Louisiana, and Tennessee.

Lincoln's position upset members of the more radical wing of his party, who could not understand the president's constitutional restraint. In a scathing manifesto published in August, Representative Davis and Senator Wade even questioned Lincoln's sincerity in declaring himself in favor of a constitutional amendment abolishing slavery: "We curiously inquire on what his expectation rests, after the [negative] vote of the House of Representatives at the recent session, and in the face of the political complexion of more than enough of the States to prevent the possibility of its adoption within any reasonable time; and why he did not indulge his sincere hopes with so large an installment of the blessing as his approval of the bill would have secured."[12]

Lincoln's endorsement of the amendment came as a major shift in a number of ways. The amendment required wholly federal and immediate emancipation, and its enactment would eliminate any need for gradual or state-based emancipation schemes. Moreover, Lincoln had by now abandoned talk of colonization. Perhaps the experience of black and white soldiers fighting together for the Union, as well as petitions such as the one presented to him by black Louisianans in March 1864, led Lincoln to shift from concern that the two races could not get along to thinking about how they could.

It is unclear the extent to which the amendment factored into the 1864 election. On one hand, with the House having voted down the amendment, most campaign discussion concentrated on other matters. Many Republicans focused on talking about loyalty and restoration of the Union, casting Democrats as copperheads and traitors, and avoiding the issue of race in tight contests. Representative Ashley talked about "man's equality before the law" in his race and almost lost. The amendment's defeat in Congress also eliminated it as an issue for state legislative elections, though it would be these state legislators who would vote on ratification. In fact, in January 1865 Representative Robert Mallory of Kentucky opposed the amendment in part because the state legislators charged with voting on ratification had not been elected with the issue in mind. Mallory claimed it would be unfair for the people not to have expressed their will on that level. Moreover, what Lincoln most needed in order to win reelection were military victories, which came when Admiral David Farragut took control of Mobile Bay in August and General Sherman took Atlanta in early September. Lincoln's assistant John G. Nicolay wrote to one editor, "The Atlanta victory alone, ought to win the Presidential contest for us." On the other hand, the Republican platform called for abolition by constitutional amendment. While the election of 1864 may not have been an explicit, one-issue referendum on the amendment, it was clear where the two parties stood.[13]

Lincoln, meanwhile, maintained his consistency on the slavery issue during his reelection bid. In July, Lincoln addressed putative Confederate emissaries in Canada by issuing his "To Whom It May Concern" letter. In it, Lincoln made clear he would discuss peace only on the basis of "the integrity of the whole Union, and the abandonment of slavery." Some people realized the political danger of the announcement, as New York City lawyer George Templeton Strong identified Lincoln's statement as a "blunder" that "may cost him the election. By declaring that abandonment of slavery is a fundamental article in any negotiation for peace and settlement, he has given the disaffected and discontented a weapon that doubles their power of mischief."[14]

Seward, gauging public opinion, issued a more ambiguous statement in September. Speaking in Auburn, New York, after the fall of Atlanta, Seward announced, "*When the insurgents shall have disbanded their armies, and laid down their arms, the war will instantly cease—and all the war measures then existing, including those which affect slavery, will cease also.*" According to Seward, when that happened, all questions, including those affecting slavery, would "*pass over to the arbitrament of courts of law, and to the councils of legislation.*" In his speech, reprinted as a campaign pamphlet, Seward spoke of courts and legislatures addressing slavery, not of Lincoln's pronouncement identifying emancipation in the Confederate states as a prerequisite for peace. Lincoln sensed the political pragmatism of allowing Seward's statements to dangle as possibilities and did not refute them.[15]

The *Continental Monthly* in September 1864, meanwhile, challenged readers to support the amendment: "Ought liberty to become part of the supreme law of the land? Ought the idea of the nation to be now, at last, incorporated into the law of the nation, and so made a fixed fact of the nation's history?" Absolving the Founders on the issue, the essay noted, "The way is opened to us, as it was not to our fathers, to remove the curse from our borders," and the "time has come to complete the unity of the Constitution, and make the

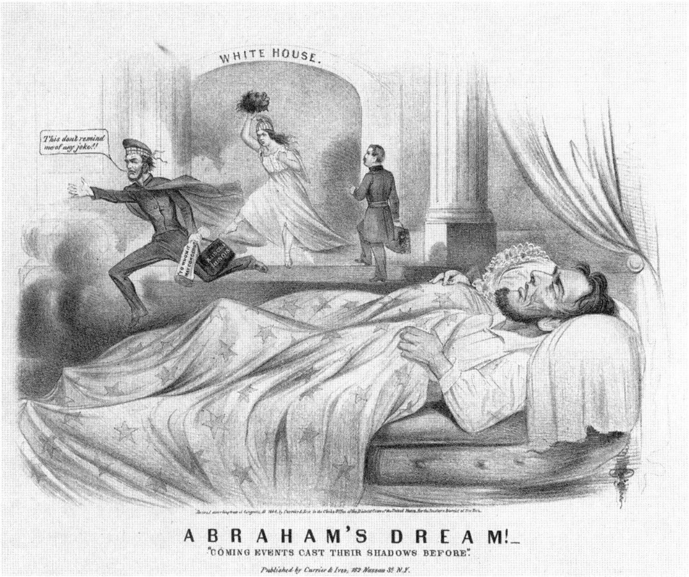

Lincoln having a nightmare about the election of 1864: George B. McClellan enters the White House as Columbia kicks out the president, throwing at him the severed head of a black man. Lincoln exclaims, "This don't remind me of any joke!!," and wears clothing meant to allude to his trip to Washington, D.C., as president-elect in 1861. Lincoln also carries his July 1864 "To Whom It May Concern" letter, in which he made the "abandonment of slavery" a prerequisite for ending the war. "Abraham's Dream!," Currier and Ives (probably drawn by Louis Maurer), 1864. Library of Congress.

ideal purpose of it, as stated in the preamble." From London, Robert John Walker, a former Democratic senator from Mississippi and Polk's secretary of the Treasury now serving as a financial agent for the Union, wrote a letter in favor of Lincoln's reelection that also supported the amendment. Walker asked, "If . . . Slavery is the great enemy of the Union, and was the sole cause of the rebellion, why not extirpate the *cause* of the war? Why not remove what may remain of Slavery after the war is ended, by the proposed amendment, as recommended by Mr. Lincoln?" Walker predicted, "This measure, which would settle finally and forever the Slavery question, will succeed at an early period, if Mr. Lincoln should be reelected."[16]

On the other hand, some Lincoln supporters talked about emancipation, but not necessarily the amendment. In a speech in Massachusetts, Patrick R. Guiney, an Irish-born lawyer severely wounded at the Battle of the Wilderness, called slavery "the strength of the rebellion." Guiney identified slavery as an embarrassing contradiction to the United States' self-identification as the worldwide beacon of republican values, noting that "the American people, who should have been the first in the race for liberty, yet were the last," and he reminded his audience that the Democrats desired no more than the restoration of the Union while Republicans wanted to end "a great crime against the human race." Yet Guiney never mentioned in his speech the amendment linked to the election, which was surprising considering that he was an attorney and likely interested in constitutional issues.[17]

A national convention of black men held in upstate New York in early October had a different approach: it went beyond emancipation to call for equal rights. In an address to the American people, the convention delivered a stinging critique of the tepid Republican position regarding black rights, claiming that while the Democrats threatened black people with their position on slavery, Republicans imperiled them with their passivity. The message expressed the concern black people had that some of the party might even waver as to abolition. Referring to the Republican platform and Lincoln's "To Whom It May Concern" letter as good signs, the delegates still feared "that the Republican party, though a party composed of the best men of the country, is not prepared to make the abolition of slavery, in all the Rebel States, a consideration precedent to the re-establishment of the Union. However antislavery in sentiment the President may be, and however disposed he may be to continue the war till slavery is abolished, it is plain that in this he would not be sustained by his party."[18]

As proof, the delegates cited the efforts of some Republican newspapers trying to explain away Lincoln's "To Whom It May Concern" letter. Seward's Auburn speech provided the delegates with even more unease because it raised the possibility of the federal government making peace with the rebels but also with slavery. In a context where Congress had declined to pass an abolition amendment and the Supreme Court only a few years earlier had issued its *Dred Scott* ruling (although Lincoln had appointed four new justices since then, and soon would appoint a fifth: Salmon P. Chase as chief justice), the only hope the delegates saw for ending slavery was for the "Rebels, in their madness," to "continue to make war upon the Government" so that they would become "destitute of men, money, and the munitions of war" and "divested of their slaves also." The address ended by imploring Americans to abolish slavery and then to enfranchise black men.[19]

The 1864 Democratic national platform ignored the amendment and did not explicitly address slavery, though voters knew that a Democratic victory probably meant the death of the amendment and an end to federal emancipation efforts. Instead, the platform criticized Lincoln's conduct of the war and claimed he violated the Constitution with his Emancipation Proclamation and other wartime policies. A message during the campaign from several prominent Democrats, signed by men such as Representative Daniel W. Voorhees of Indiana, Democratic vice presidential nominee George H. Pendleton (also a representative from Ohio), and former representative Clement Vallandigham of Ohio, called on people "who are for the Constitution as it is and the Union as it was" to unite with them. Robert C. Winthrop, a former Whig speaker of the House of Representatives who now supported Democratic candidate George B. McClellan, in October 1864 delivered a speech in which he announced, "We want the Constitution of Washington, and Franklin, and Hamilton, and Madison, and Jay, without addition and without diminution."[20]

While he monitored his own reelection campaign, Lincoln closely watched congressional races with particular concern about obtaining enough votes to pass the amendment (an issue the *New York Times* had raised in mid-June 1864). Lincoln received alarming reports of a chaotic situation in Missouri in the months prior to the election, including murder, destruction of property, and discord among different Republicans. He sent his private secretary, John G. Nicolay, to provide a firsthand report on the situation in the state. Nicolay arrived in St. Louis by October 8, reporting a few days later, "Things are in a pretty bad tangle." By October 18, Nicolay wrote Lincoln, "There is little else than personal animosity, and the usual eagerness to appropriate the spoils, that is left to prevent a full and harmonious

An 1864 election cartoon in which Lincoln exclaims, "No peace without Abolition!" and Confederate president Jefferson Davis insists, "No peace without Separation!" while George B. McClellan tries to stop them from tearing apart a map of the United States by asserting, "The Union must be preserved at all hazards!" "The True Issue or 'That[']s What[']s the Matter,'" Currier and Ives, 1864. Library of Congress.

combination of all the Union voters of Missouri." Nicolay highlighted the state's first congressional district, representing St. Louis, as a particular concern and reported that he had "urged upon the factions . . . that their quarrel there ought not to be permitted to lose us the Congressman there—that if we continued to make gains as we had done in Indiana, Ohio and Pennsylvania we should get a two-thirds vote in the House and thus be able to pass the Constitutional Amendment about Slavery. They acknowledged the importance of the matter and will I think unite on a third candidate and elect him." As of November 2, a Republican informant wrote Nicolay that the Unconditional Unionist and Radical candidates "waged with great bitterness" their campaign against each other, but he erred when he reported, "The Copperhead candidate is regarded as out of the question"—Democrat John Hogan won the election, but the other eight members of Missouri's delegation to the House would be Republicans.[21]

Lincoln also eagerly watched emancipation developments in Maryland and used events there to make a number of public pronouncements in support of abolition. Lincoln knew that a Border State abolishing slavery on its own would send a powerful message to Congress and the American people. On October 10 Lincoln responded to the collector of customs at Baltimore, Henry W. Hoffman, who asked for a word from Lincoln to be used at a public meeting in Baltimore that evening to help secure ratification of a state constitution abolishing slavery. Lincoln replied, "I presume the only feature of the instrument, about which there is serious controversy, is that which provides for the extinction of slavery. It needs not to be a secret, and I presume it is no secret, that I wish success to this provision. I desire it on every consideration. I wish all men to be free. I wish the material prosperity of the already free which I feel sure the extinction of slavery would bring. I wish to see, in process of disappearing, that only thing which ever could bring this nation to civil war." Lincoln concluded, "I shall be gratified exceedingly if the good people of the State shall, by their votes, ratify the new constitution." Maryland held a referendum on October 12, 1864, the same day Chief Justice Roger Taney, a Marylander, died. On October 15 Lincoln monitored telegrams from Hoffman, including one that accurately predicted that the "soldiers vote" may "give a small majority for the Constitution." Lincoln carefully tabulated returns as they arrived and asked Hoffman to meet with him that night in Washington. By a margin of a couple hundred votes, secured by the lopsided soldiers' vote in favor of it, Maryland accepted a new state constitution abolishing slavery.[22]

Lincoln on October 18 declared, "I had rather have Maryland upon that issue than have a State twice its size upon the Presidential issue; it cleans up a piece of ground." After winning reelection, Lincoln addressed the Maryland Union Committee in similar terms, claiming that he would have stipulated to lose Maryland in the presidential election to save its free constitution, "because the Presidential election comes every four years and the adoption of the constitution, being a good thing, could not be undone."[23]

On October 19 Lincoln responded to a serenade of Marylanders in a talk published in newspapers. "Most heartily do I congratulate you, and Maryland, and the nation, and the world, upon the event. I regret that it did not occur two years sooner, which I am sure would have saved to the nation more money than would have met all the private loss incident to the measure. But it has come at last." Lincoln also reiterated some of his longest held principles of constitutional fidelity and respect for the will of the people in terms reminiscent of similar statements from his First Inaugural Address.[24]

Declared ratified on October 29, the Maryland Constitution went into effect November 1. In between, Lincoln briefly addressed the Forty-Second Massachusetts Volunteer Infantry Regiment upon the expiration of its term of service, recalling how a Baltimore mob had attacked a Massachusetts regiment passing through that city in 1861. Lincoln bluntly noted, "The world has moved since then, and I congratulate you upon having a better time to-day in Baltimore than that regiment had." Lincoln added, "To-night, midnight, slavery ceases in Maryland, and this state of things in Maryland is due greatly to the soldiers."[25]

The following day, Lincoln addressed a celebratory crowd of black people who held a torchlight procession to the White House. "It is no secret that I have wished, and still do wish, mankind everywhere to be free," Lincoln began. He admitted, "It is difficult to realize that in that State, where human slavery has existed for ages, ever since a period long before any here were born—by the action of her own citizens—the soil is made forever free." Lincoln went on, "I do believe that it will result in good to the white race as well as to those who have been made free by this act of emancipation, and I hope that the time will soon come when all will see that the perpetuation of freedom for all in Maryland is best for the interests of all, though some may thereby be made to suffer temporary pecuniary loss." Specifically addressing the freedpeople, Lincoln expressed his "hope" that they would "use this great boon which has been given you to improve yourselves, both morally and intellectually," before wishing them a good night.[26]

Lincoln's statements may not have directly addressed the constitutional amendment, but his overall message continually affirmed his position, even as many Republicans remained quiet on the issue. The election resulted in more than Lincoln's victory: Republicans picked up enough seats in the House to assure that the Thirty-Ninth Congress, which could meet as early as March 1865, would be able to pass a resolution proposing the abolition amendment to the states.

Republicans now cast the election as a referendum in support of a constitutional amendment. Days after the election, Frederick Douglass delivered an address in Rochester, New York, summarizing its importance. Besides determining "life or death to the nation," Douglass told his audience, the election reflected "an endorsement, full and complete, of all the leading measures inaugurated by the present Administration, looking to the final extirpation of slavery from our land." Douglass declared that its result "means that the Constitution of the United States shall be so changed that slavery can never again exist in any part of the United States." Douglass noted that opponents attacked the war as a failure and charged the

An 1864 election broadside contrasting Lincoln's support for free labor, as he shakes the hand of a worker while black and white children exit a schoolhouse, with George B. McClellan's tolerance for slavery, as he shakes hands with Confederate president Davis in front of a slave auction. "Union and Liberty! And Union and Slavery!," M. W. Seibert, 1864. Library of Congress.

Union party as being "an abolition party" and "a negro party," but now, he claimed, "the people heard it all, and saw it all, and have accepted it all," that "the people have answered, 'we are not ashamed of the negro.'"[27]

William Lloyd Garrison wrote a fellow abolitionist that "Mr. Lincoln's re-election is certainly the death-warrant of the whole slave system, and indicates that we are very near the day of jubilee." Garrison declared, "I have no doubt that, among the earliest acts of the approaching session of Congress, the adoption of the contemplated anti-slavery amendment of the Constitution will be successful," and then the amendment may be "promptly submitted for popular ratification." In Brooklyn, John Jay (grandson of the Supreme Court chief justice of the same name) predicted after Lincoln's reelection, "With the suppression of the rebellion and the reconstruction of our old Union there will come, throughout the sunny South, by this rebel war and an amendment to the Constitution, the substitution of free homesteads for slave plantations, and what a blessed vista that thought opens to the imagination!"[28]

With his actions and his words, Lincoln helped shift public opinion on the matter of slavery, as Garrison had noted. Now, with his final campaign behind him, Lincoln could turn his energy toward getting Congress to pass an amendment resolution to be sent to the states for ratification. Lincoln had reasons for making sure the current Congress did so, and he would use his reelection as the mandate of the people in order to get the resolution passed.

CHAPTER SIX

GETTING THE AMENDMENT RESOLUTION PASSED

"'*If slavery is not wrong, nothing is wrong.*' Thus simply and truthfully has spoken our worthy Chief Magistrate," began Representative James M. Ashley on January 6, 1865, when he called up his motion for the House to reconsider its June 1864 vote on the proposed amendment. The Lincoln quote came from an April 1864 letter to a Kentucky editor in which Lincoln declared, "I am naturally anti-slavery," as well as that he had "never understood that the Presidency conferred upon me an unrestricted right to act officially upon this judgment and feeling on slavery." Lincoln in the letter affirmed his fidelity to the Constitution in all official matters, "that, to this day, I have done no official act in mere deference to my abstract judgment and feeling on slavery." By now, however, Lincoln had settled on the way to end slavery nationwide within the boundaries of the Constitution—by amending the document. Republican representative Godlove S. Orth of Indiana followed Ashley, calling the recent election a "popular verdict . . . expressed in unmistakable language, and he who is willing to bow to the voice of those whom for the time being he represents in this Hall, cannot doubt the action the people now expect at his hands."[1]

Shortly after his victory, Lincoln urged the same Congress that had failed to pass the abolition amendment to do so now. "Although the present is the same Congress, and nearly the same members," Lincoln acknowledged in his Annual Message dated December 6, 1864,

"I venture to recommend the reconsideration and passage of the measure at the present session." As a practical matter, Lincoln recognized, "the abstract question is not changed," but the election results meant "almost certainly, that the next Congress will pass the measure if this does not." As it now was a matter of when, not if, the proposed amendment would get sent to the states for ratification, Lincoln asked, why not sooner rather than later?[2]

Lincoln argued that the 1864 national election had created a mandate on the issue: "It is the voice of the people now, for the first time, heard upon the question." Lincoln linked passage of the amendment with the "nearly unanimous" support by the people for the "common end" of maintaining the Union, holding that, "among the means to secure that end, such will, through the election, is most clearly declared in favor of such constitutional amendment." According to Lincoln, "The most reliable indication of public purpose in this country is derived through our popular elections," and thus he called for "deference . . . to the will of the majority."[3]

Ashley, the amendment bill's manager in the House, foresaw a battle going into debate on the measure, however. Radical Republicans might push for an amendment that emphasized equal rights and defined what freedom meant in more explicit detail, but such a measure would be harder to pass out of Congress and get ratified by the states. War Democrats and moderate Republicans may have supported abolition for various reasons but not a definition of black rights, and many of them envisioned an America where chattel slavery no longer existed but racial discrimination did. Civil and political rights, they believed, were issues for states to determine. Other Republicans, however, held the view that emancipation required equality before the law and integrating black people into a fully free labor society. For pragmatic reasons, Republicans in Congress held off on this discussion, however, and kept silent on the matter of political rights, remaining vague on what the amendment meant so as to secure its passage.[4]

On the other hand, many Democrats continued their strong opposition to the amendment. Some of them feared that the amendment would preclude any peace efforts and thus perpetuate the war. Others held that the amendment proposal itself exceeded the scope of what

Article V allowed to be amended and that it destroyed federalism by addressing slavery in the states. Moreover, while events in Maryland and Missouri (a constitutional convention scheduled to meet there in January 1865 would vote to abolish slavery) may have signaled victories for slavery's opponents, these developments also emphasized the possibility that state-based emancipation precluded the need to alter the Constitution. Some Democrats maintained that the amendment wrongfully destroyed property, albeit in human beings. In the previous session, Democratic representative Fernando Wood of New York, one of the staunchest critics of the measure, claimed that the amendment would destroy "individual property," and he argued that the Constitution could not justly be amended to "appropriate private property without due compensation, or confiscate it without the formality of trial and condemnation." Around Christmas 1864, Ashley calculated that 108 members were ready to support an amendment resolution in the next session, 14 short of what he needed. Lincoln, who in his draft for a February 1861 speech in Pittsburgh wrote that Congress should craft and pass legislation with little involvement from the executive, now dove into the legislative process with vigor.[5]

Much of Lincoln's personal attention focused on the Border States. The day after Lincoln's Annual Message, former Missouri newspaper editor Abel R. Corbin met with Lincoln to discuss a plan for securing votes by two lame-duck Missouri congressmen who had voted against the amendment in June: Unionists Austin A. King (a former Democrat who was defeated for reelection) and James S. Rollins (a former Whig who chose not to run again). The judge of the Western District of Missouri, Robert W. Wells, had died on September 22, 1864, and several weeks later, Missouri senator John B. Henderson urged Lincoln to appoint attorney and newspaper editor Arnold Krekel to the vacant judgeship "at once." King, meanwhile, wrote Attorney General Edward Bates in November that he wanted the position himself, asking him to use his influence to obtain "an office in the gift of the President."[6]

Corbin now advised Lincoln to use the position in a way that would make King and Rollins eager to please Lincoln so as to influence his choice of Wells's successor. On December 8, 1864, Corbin wrote Lincoln to reiterate his advice that he "*not fill, nor promise*" the post until after the vote on the amendment. "I propose to *promise* no body *anything*," Corbin counseled, "but I wish to have 'a serpent hanging' up 'on a pole' in the sight of all." If Lincoln followed this advice, Corbin assured, "I will please you by the result," adding that "your amendment *shall* pass. I can [also] get you some New York votes." Corbin also noted that a two-thirds vote meant two-thirds of those members present, so that "*absenteeism*" could be used "to insure your triumph *in time* to secure the action of the State Legislatures *prior* to the expiration of your First Term." Rollins and King both voted for the amendment. In March 1865, Lincoln appointed and the Senate confirmed Krekel to the position after Senator Benjamin Gratz Brown of Missouri seconded Henderson's endorsement.[7]

In the 1880s, Rollins also recounted that Lincoln several times had personally "expressed his deep anxiety" to him regarding passage of the amendment. Rollins's recollections very likely contain a kernel of truth wrapped in some embellishment. According to Rollins, Lincoln asked to meet him at the White House, during which the president explained that if enough members of the Border State delegation united so as to pass the amendment, it would help speed the war's end by showing the Confederates that they never would receive help from that quarter. Thus, Lincoln continued, "I have sent for you, as an old Whig friend, to come and see me, that I might make an appeal to you to vote for this amendment. It is going to be very close; a few votes one way or the other will decide it." Rollins recounted that he informed Lincoln he had already decided he would vote for the amendment, even though he was one of the largest slaveholders in his county and many of his constituents were slaveholders as well. Lincoln then asked Rollins where other members of Missouri's delegation to the House stood regarding the amendment and requested that the congressman lobby those who might be persuaded to vote for it. In his account, Rollins mistakenly has Lincoln ask specifically about the position of Thomas L. Price, who had served in the prior Congress and no longer held office. According to Rollins, he began conveying Lincoln's interest to fellow Border State representatives the next day (including Price). On January 13, moreover, Rollins delivered a speech in favor of the amendment. In his account, Rollins had Lincoln a few days after passage of the amendment saying to him, "I read your speech, one night, after I had gone to bed, and it is the best speech delivered in Congress during this session."[8]

Lincoln also tried to cultivate the support of Democrats, meeting between Christmas and New Year's with two lame-duck congressmen of that party—Samuel "Sunset" Cox of Ohio (who got the nickname for his description of a sunset in an editorial) and John T. Stuart of Illinois (Lincoln's former law partner and Mary Todd's cousin). Lincoln told them he was "anxious to have our Democratic aid and vote for the proposition to amend the Constitution so as to abolish slavery." Cox promised to help, "provided a sincere effort was made for peace within the Union," and he recollected telling Lincoln he would support the amendment if that effort failed. Cox credited this meeting with influencing Lincoln to give Francis P. Blair Sr. on December 28, 1864, a pass to Richmond, an effort ultimately resulting in the Hampton Roads Conference. In a memoir published later that year, Cox wrote that he "had several interviews with party friends, at my room, with that view. I was anxious, as a Democrat, and with a view to the upbuilding of the party I cherished, to drive this question, which had become abstract by the death of slavery through powder and ball, from the political arena." Cox earlier in December had privately suggested to Manton M. Marble, editor of a major national Democratic organ, the *New York World*, that Democrats should "vote to '*eliminate*' the 'Slavery question' out of our politics, for the purpose of future success."[9]

A little harder to verify is a story written by Representative Isaac N. Arnold, who in 1866 recounted that a Democrat had a brother mortally wounded at Chancellorsville and that "Mr. Lincoln's kindness to him while in the hospital at Washington, visiting him, and relieving every want, won the heart of the Congressman." According to Arnold, Lincoln said to the representative during a reception, "Your brother died to save the Republic from death by the slaveholders rebellion. I wish you could see it to be your duty to vote for the Constitutional amendment ending slavery," and the member thus voted for the amendment.[10]

If Arnold's recollection is accurate, it seems this discussion likely would have occurred during debate on the first House vote on the amendment in 1864, and in his book he recounted the story in the section right after his recollection of his 1864 New Year's Day conversation with Lincoln. Only four Democrats voted for the amendment that time—Moses F. Odell and John A. Griswold of New York, Joseph Baily of Pennsylvania, and Ezra Wheeler of Wisconsin. An only son, Griswold ran for reelection in 1864 as a Republican. While one of Baily's brothers had died on a business trip to Philadelphia, his other three brothers still lived at the time of the voting on the amendment. Wheeler delivered a speech in favor of the amendment on June 14, 1864, but never mentioned a family member giving his life for the Union (he did want to revise the proposed amendment so that it would apply to Kentucky, Missouri, Maryland, and Delaware ten years after ratification). While *Harper's Weekly* in June 1862 published an article mentioning Odell caring for soldiers wounded at First Bull Run, it did not mention a brother serving in the army. Wounded at Chancellorsville, a Private William Odell served in the 124th New York, though it is unknown whether he was related to the congressman or if Lincoln paid him a visit.[11]

In addition to Lincoln's personal outreach, Secretary of State Seward gathered a team to help lobby for the amendment. It is difficult to know exactly how much Lincoln knew of these efforts, or what he thought of them, but Seward likely kept the president closely informed, and at least one letter exists in which a member of the lobby provided a direct update to Lincoln. In June 1865 Lincoln's former postmaster general, Montgomery Blair, implied in a letter to President Andrew Johnson that Lincoln knew about Seward's efforts, whether at the time or shortly thereafter.[12]

Seward's acquaintance, William N. Bilbo of Nashville, seems to have taken the lead of the group. A lawyer, speculator, and former Whig, Bilbo had good connections with political figures in the South as well as in New York. Known for wearing flashy waistcoats, Bilbo originally supported the Confederacy before an abrupt turnaround in 1864, when he arrived in New York and pledged himself to the Union cause. A number of other well-connected men assisted him. John W. Forney, an important figure in Pennsylvania's prewar

Democratic Party and proprietor of the *Philadelphia Press* and *Washington Chronicle*, had become a Republican and served as secretary of the Senate from 1861 to 1868. Emmanuel B. Hart served a term in Congress as a Democrat before President Buchanan appointed him to the position of surveyor of the port of New York, an important patronage post that he held from 1857 to 1861. Robert W. Latham, a self-described "old friend" of the secretary of state, focused on promoting Seward's career, not Lincoln's. In early 1864 Latham predicted to Seward that Lincoln could not be renominated and advised, "The Election of the next President is in your hands. *Please, do not throw it away!*" Latham had lobbied Congress before the war, earning allegations of unscrupulous behavior in the process, and he had helped Seward in connection with the establishment of West Virginia's government. Richard Schell, a charming and likable Wall Street speculator and Tammany Hall Democrat, enjoyed a friendship and frequent correspondence with Seward.[13]

In late November 1864, Bilbo sought and obtained an interview with Lincoln in Washington, D.C. Democrat Homer A. Nelson, a former judge in Dutchess County, New York, now serving his single term in Congress, introduced Bilbo to the president. Nelson would prove valuable to Bilbo's efforts despite an initial hesitance to get involved. Shortly after this meeting, Bilbo began working on the Thirteenth Amendment, though he directed almost all of his correspondence to Seward, not to Lincoln.[14]

Bilbo first visited Thurlow Weed in New York, though that meeting proved unsuccessful. Bilbo wrote Seward that he had met with Weed "as you directed," but "we had mistaken our man"; Weed "was no Abolitionist" and "would not have any thing to do with it." While Bilbo expressed that he was "surprised" by the outcome of the meeting, he assured Seward he was "not less determined. I promised you the requisite votes, and neither energy[,] time or money shall be wanting upon my part to attain our end." By mid-December, Bilbo reported to Seward from New York City that he had "succeeded in procuring the requisite number of Democratic votes to pass the measure so dear to your heart" and that he planned to leave the following night to confer with Seward in Washington.[15]

By December 20, Bilbo reported to Seward from Washington that one of his helpers, George O. Jones, an Albany lobbyist and agent of an upstate New York railroad, had met with two important New York Democrats, Governor Horatio Seymour and Dean Richmond, leader of the Albany Regency political machine. According to Bilbo, both men said that if they served in Congress, they "could not vote for the Amendment," but "they will not advise against voting for it!" While Seymour and Richmond probably expressed concern that the amendment would adjust the doctrine and practice of federalism, Bilbo informed Seward that they had admitted, "No party North can maintain its political status that opposes it. Jones says that the New York Democrats will suffice to carry it." Bilbo met Seward at the secretary's home that night, and Jones, staying in Willard's Hotel with Bilbo, postponed a meeting between himself, Nelson, and Seward until the following morning. By December 23, Bilbo and Nelson had returned to New York City, where they roomed together.[16]

Meanwhile, on January 7, 1865, Latham met with "Sunset" Cox (and reported to Seward that the congressman planned to call on him) and editor Thomas B. Florence of the Democratic *Constitutional Union*. By January 9 Latham had also conferred with John S. Carlile, a Unionist from Virginia who voted with Democrats in the Senate, and Kansas Radical Republican senator Samuel C. Pomeroy. While Carlile had not voted on the amendment when it was before the Senate, Latham likely assumed he would have sway with Democrats in the House but reported to Seward that he "has not the courage, to press the resolution through." Latham concluded, "I have no doubt about passing *it. Money will certainly* do it, if patriotism fails."[17]

By January 10, 1865, Bilbo wrote Seward from Washington, D.C., that "the discussions in Congress, are not aiding us," reporting that "the most strenuous efforts are made by the Leaders of the Democracy, to unite every member in the House against the Amendment." Bilbo reported, "They beset [Nelson] on all sides," adding, "I can not do anything with Fernando Woods [*sic*]." By January 11, the *New York Times* reporter in Washington concurred that opposition to the amendment resolution seemed strong: "It is to-day feared that there is no hope of the passage in the House of the Constitutional

Amendment abolishing slavery." On the other hand, in his January 10 letter, Bilbo assured Seward, "All of our parts should work today." That same day, Bilbo reported to vice president–elect Andrew Johnson "to night [*sic*] the Rubicon is passed," and he predicted passage of the amendment by several votes, helped by absentees and after the application of "some 'Knock Down' *material* arguments." Bilbo planned to confer with Seward and then return to New York City on January 14.[18]

Latham, Forney, and Hart kept in touch with Seward as well. By January 12 Hart asked Seward, through Latham, to have Weed to come to Washington. Weed did, in fact, arrive in Washington shortly thereafter. In April 1865, an upstate New York paper commented on Weed's conversion from opposing abolition, though he did little else to assist the cause. Bilbo in November 1865 even wrote Seward, "I freely forgive [Weed] for refusing to aid us in the passage of the Constitutional Amendment."[19]

In the middle of these efforts, on January 12, "Sunset" Cox delivered a major speech refuting one of the main arguments of Democratic opponents: that slavery stood outside the reach of the Constitution's amendment power. The House debate focused on that issue on January 10 and 11, and remarks by Representative George Pendleton of Ohio, a Peace Democrat and McClellan's running mate, serve as an example of the argument some representatives made that the Article V amendment power did not extend to slavery. Pendleton insisted, "Authority over the status of its citizens belongs to each State," and "you cannot, under the power of amendment, contravene the letter and spirit of the Constitution . . . you cannot destroy the liberties of the States; . . . you cannot decide the status of the citizens of the States." Pendleton went so far to say that, "if you attempt to impose that amendment upon the dissenting States by force, it will be their right to resist you by force."[20]

Cox had already met with Lincoln in late December and with Latham on January 7. On January 10, Cox announced to the House that the American people had, pursuant to the amendment power, "the right to do anything; to erect a monarchy in this country; to make the king of Dahomey . . . the king of this country." Now,

Cox defended the broad power of amendment in a more developed oration, calling Article V "an element of democracy" and a credit to the Founders that they "did not tie the hands of the children nor shackle their liberties by laws so irrevocable that no mode of change was allowed." According to Cox, "An amendment is a safety-valve, or governor, upon the engine of State. A State without it, is in perpetual danger of violent revolution." But, Cox observed, "amendment is a peaceful, legal, and salutary revolution," and he called it "the beauty of our system of written constitutions that . . . any irregularity may be corrected without breaking the machine or impairing the movement." Cox added that the process of amendment provided a check on intemperate decisions, having to filter through two-thirds of both houses of Congress or two-thirds of the state legislatures calling for a convention, followed by ratification by three-fourths of the states. "Am I answered that it is undemocratic to allow this power? I answer, it is only undemocratic to disallow it." Cox thus went further than did Ashley, who had stated, "Congress may propose and three fourths of the States may adopt, any amendment, republican in its character and consistent with the continued existence of the nation [save for two caveats in Article V]."[21]

On January 31, 1865, the day the House passed the amendment resolution, Lincoln wrote Cox, "Thank you for the speech. I sought it for the humor said to be in it; but while it meets expectations in that respect, it has a far higher merit, so far as I can judge by the hasty glance I have only found time to give it." While it is possible the speech to which Lincoln referred was one delivered by Cox a few days earlier opposing a House resolution that would have given the heads of executive departments seats on the congressional floor, it is tempting to think that Lincoln alluded to a copy of Cox's January 12 speech. No correspondence from Cox on the issue has been found, nor did he mention the matter in his 1865 memoir in which he reprinted both speeches.[22]

By January 14 Bilbo had retreated from his earlier assessment to the vice president–elect and now reported to Johnson from Washington that the vote on the amendment had been postponed for two weeks because "we need *two* votes more *for* the Bill, and three

Absentees." Bilbo urged Johnson, still serving as Tennessee's military governor, to move along the state convention there so that the state's ten congressional votes could be elected and arrive to "help us pass the Amendment."[23]

Bilbo returned to New York, where he was arrested as a Confederate spy. Lincoln swiftly ordered Major General John A. Dix to release Bilbo, who by January 23 wrote Seward that someone had made the accusation out of "unmitigated malice" or "total ignorance of my sentiments." Bilbo added that, according to George O. Jones, Horatio Seymour (whose term as governor had expired) said about the amendment, "Now he was perfectly indifferent as to its passage and that he would not offer any opposition to it."[24]

By late January, efforts seem to have focused on winning the support of the influential anti-Lincoln, pro-Democratic *New York World*. "Sunset" Cox had written the newspaper's editor, Manton Marble, in early December that slavery should be eliminated for the good of the Democratic Party, and in mid-December 1864 the paper had signaled Democrats they could act as they wished on the subject of slavery. By the end of December, however, the paper argued that Democratic congressmen should vote against the amendment, though not speak against it, under the assumption that delaying the measure would induce the Confederate states to return to the Union so as to defeat the measure in the following Congress. On January 9 the paper further criticized the amendment because, in its current form and without additional constitutional amendments, black people would face "intolerable oppression." The *World* did not express its disapproval out of concern for the rights of black people but instead to raise a warning that additional changes to the Constitution—and revisions to federalism—would follow it.[25]

On January 23 another member of the secretary of state's lobby team, Richard Schell, wrote Seward from New York that he had met with Samuel L. M. Barlow, a wealthy attorney and chief strategist for McClellan's presidential campaign who also held a controlling interest in the *World*. Schell reported that Barlow "promised to have an article written" in favor of the amendment, adding that Barlow owed him a favor: Schell had made him $10,000, and he had paid the money during the meeting. Doing so, Schell thought, "will give me controul [*sic*] over him," but he added that they "shall know in two days as he told me he would submit to me the article tomorrow."[26]

A few days later, Bilbo wrote Seward on January 26 that he had just met with Manton Marble at the office of the *World*. Around the same time, Marble received a letter from Richmond of the Albany Regency, asking the editor not to make the amendment a "party question" and to allow "each member of Congress . . . [to] vote according to his own disposition." According to Bilbo, Marble told him "that on Friday or Saturday he would write an article declaring it was no test of Democracy to vote 'for' or 'against'" the amendment, "rather indicating to its party that they had better vote for it. The editor said to me it was his wish rather that they should vote for it." Bilbo suggested having the article copied in Forney's pro-Lincoln *Washington Chronicle*, "to ease some of the conscientious scruples of some Democrats," and asked Seward to inform Nelson of these developments "so that he can use it with Democrats."[27]

Bilbo wrote Lincoln directly that same day. After expressing gratitude that Lincoln intervened to have him released from arrest (adding, "I may be justly charged of being impulsive, defiant, and precipitant [*sic*], but never as a hyporcrite [*sic*] or a spy"), Bilbo reported, "I have at last succeeded this evening through my friends in prevaling [*sic*] upon the 'World' the organ of the Democracy to declare on Saturday or Friday that to vote *for* or *against* the 'Amendment' clause on Tuesday next was no test of Democracy, and rather indirectly to advise the Democracy to vote for it. I was thus promised this evening by its Editor[.] So you need not have any apprehension now upon its passage. Gov[.] Seymour has declared that he had no interest upon the subject, and if it passed he would have no regrets. This he declared to George W. Jones a former Dem member of congress whom I sent to test him." Bilbo added that Nelson "has been indefatigable in his assiduous efforts to procure other Democrats to vote for it." Bilbo closed with an assurance that the amendment "will pass and thus I will have discharged my obligations to you & Mr[.] Seward as an old line Whig, and my paramount obligations to eternal justice and an universal humanity."[28]

Montgomery Blair also wrote Barlow several letters urging him to support the amendment. Blair, a former Jacksonian Democrat, and Seward, a former Whig, could not stand each other, and Blair undertook his initiative independently of the Seward lobby. Blair saw the amendment as an opportunity to unite Democrats and conservative Republicans, leaving Radical Republicans and their concern with black equality as outliers. Although a friend of the president, Blair diverged from Lincoln and Seward in this regard; they sought to keep the Republicans united through the amendment, including Radicals who increasingly discussed black rights (even though Lincoln and Seward did not like their venom toward the Confederate states). Blair saw the amendment as an opportunity to marginalize the Radical Republicans who had a hand in pushing him out of his office as postmaster general in September 1864.[29]

The *World* remained silent on the amendment issue. Barlow later expressed to "Sunset" Cox that he felt the measure would hamper reunion and intrude on matters meant to be controlled by the states. After the amendment resolution passed, Bilbo lamented that the newspaper "disappointed us" after it had promised to publish an article "giving the measure an indirect support," but acknowledged, "Perhaps its silence achieved as much for its support." Bilbo also recounted a lengthy meeting he had with Seymour the previous week, when New York's now ex-governor said that when he "heard of prominent Democrats of N York favoring this measure, he had resolved not to interfere—not to write a letter to any Member of Congress upon the subject, nor to express any opinion to others upon the subject—that it was no test of Democratic loyalty to vote for or against the measure—that he was opposed [to] making it a party question &c." According to Bilbo, "It was Gov[.] Seymour that silenced the 'World,' which paper at first tried to make it a party question to defeat it." Bilbo asked that Lincoln and Seward "not forget" his team, which included Jones, Schell, Hart, and two members of the staff of the *New York Herald*, among others, all of whom "assisted me greatly," and he noted, "Of the Members of Congress by far the most efficient was Judge Nelson who at first would not kindly listen to me."[30]

Montgomery Blair had a different view. Writing to Andrew Johnson in June 1865, Blair said "through [Dean Richmond and his Albany Regency wing of the War Democrats] we carried the Constitutional amendment," continuing, "I have always stood well with them, & beleive [*sic*] had some influence in persuading them to go the Amendment which they did on exclusively patriotic & party considerations, & yet I know that Mr. Seward made Lincoln believe that he had carried that Amendment by Corruption. The only man so influenced was Anson Herrick whose vote was paid for by an apt [appointment] & was not needed for we had a dozen more votes that were not cast for it that would have been cast if they had been needed."[31]

Lincoln and his allies expended a large amount of political capital making sure the House approved the resolution before the Thirty-Eighth Congress adjourned. Everyone knew that Lincoln could simply call a special session of Congress to pass the amendment after the Thirty-Eighth Congress adjourned on March 3. The *New York Times* raised the possibility on January 8, 1865, and Republican representative Josiah B. Grinnell of Iowa made the same observation on the House floor two days later. This possibility gives rise to an alternate line of events had the Thirty-Eighth Congress declined to pass the amendment. Reconstruction would have developed very differently because, had Lincoln convened a special session, Congress likely would have been in session upon his assassination, preempting the period of presidential Reconstruction under Johnson from April to December 1865.[32]

Practical reasons caused Lincoln to place such importance on the Thirty-Eighth Congress passing the amendment. Lincoln saw the amendment as undermining hope for the rebellion, especially because it would by necessity show Democratic support and thus demonstrate that ending slavery went beyond Republican support. Moreover, ratification by some of the slaveholding states that remained in the Union—it seemed likely that Maryland and Missouri at least would vote in favor in light of recent events in both states—would reiterate to the Confederates that the Border States would not join them.

Finally, the sooner Congress sent the amendment to the states, the sooner the issue would be out of Lincoln's hands in regard to peace talks. Lincoln could then truthfully say to any Confederate peace envoys that the matter now rested with the American people pursuant to the ratification process. As to this last point, Representative James G. Blaine of Maine noted Lincoln's fear that as the war neared an end, the desire for reunion might trump enactment of measures "essential to the future safety and strength of the National Government." Lincoln wanted the matter resolved now to preclude that possibility.[33]

CHAPTER SEVEN

THE FINAL VOTE

The House convened at noon on January 31, 1865, and, after an opening prayer and some other business, turned to what would be the final debate regarding the amendment. Representative James M. Ashley first had three Democrats who had opposed the amendment the previous June, but now supported it, deliver messages on the floor. The clerk read a short statement by Representative Archibald McAllister of Pennsylvania citing the failure of peace missions and explaining that he now planned to vote "against the cornerstone of the southern confederacy." Next, Representative Alexander Coffroth of Pennsylvania affirmed his allegiance to the Democratic Party but indicated he planned to vote for the amendment so as to remove the issue that placed the Republicans in power. Addressing any Democratic criticism, Coffroth added, "I assure them I do that only which my conscience sanctions and my sense of duty demands."[1]

After a fellow Pennsylvania representative, Democrat William H. Miller, rose to repudiate McAllister's and Coffroth's statements, Representative Anson Herrick of New York, also a Democrat, announced that the amendment had been part of the Republican platform approved "by a large majority" and that he was "now disposed to bow in submission to that popular decree." Military victories and "the presidential election . . . have necessarily exercised an important influence over the public mind," and the "rejection by the people at the polls of the proclaimed policy of the Democratic party has closed many avenues to reconciliation which remained open." Speaking to members of his party, Herrick declared, "It has been our seeming adherence to slavery, in maintaining the principle of State rights, that has, year by year, depleted our party ranks until our once powerful organization has . . . sunk into a hopeless minority in nearly every State of the Union; and every year and every day we are growing weaker and weaker in popular favor, while our opponents are strengthening, because we will not venture to cut loose from the dead carcass of negro slavery." Then some opponents of the amendment spoke but probably changed no votes.[2]

Meanwhile, another threat to the vote materialized during the debate: rumors that peace commissioners from the Confederacy drew near to Washington. Samuel "Sunset" Cox expressed concern that the amendment's passage would derail peace negotiations. Cox recounted later that year that he had wanted to purge the issue from politics for the sake of his party and that he had "fully intended" to vote for the amendment that day. Cox had stated publicly and privately he would do so "if all hope of negotiation had failed," and he had been advised by "high officials" that "no further negotiations were possible." But then Cox learned about Confederate commissioners "actually waiting to be conducted over the lines." Cox asked Ashley if the reports were true, and Ashley in turn asked Lincoln's secretary John Nicolay, who responded that he knew of no such commission. Cox pressed the issue and asked Ashley to get word from Lincoln himself.[3]

From the House floor, Ashley sent Lincoln a note via Nicolay: "The report is in circulation in the House that Peace Commissioners are on their way or are in the city, and is being used against us. If it is true, I fear we shall loose [*sic*] the bill. Please authorize me to contradict it, if not true." Lincoln received Ashley's request while in a conference with Major General Carl Schurz and swiftly responded on the note's reverse side, "So far as I know, there are no peace Commissioners in the City, or likely to be in it." Lincoln signed and dated the document and sent it back to Ashley.[4]

Ashley showed Lincoln's letter to Cox and other representatives, but Cox remained unconvinced. After hearing additional reports to the contrary, Cox "satisfied" himself that Lincoln was either "mistaken" or "ignorant" concerning the peace commission, and in the end he voted against the amendment. "Whether my vote was correct or not, it was given upon the belief that in the negotiations then about to be begun at once," Cox recalled later in 1865, "this amendment would prove an insurmountable obstacle to peace and union. Weighing in one scale the dead body of slavery, which was to be abolished by this amendment; and in the other, peace and union, and these latter, too, without slavery—could I do anything else than doubt the wisdom of an amendment which would postpone peace and imperil the Union?" Cox pointed to his speech in favor of the power to amend as the proof of his intentions.[5]

Lincoln knew exactly what was transpiring when he responded to Ashley. On December 28, 1864, Lincoln had granted Francis P. Blair Sr. a pass to "go South and return," though not as an agent of the government. Publicly, Blair wanted to retrieve some papers captured by the Confederates during a recent raid near Washington. Privately, however, Blair sought a meeting with Confederate president Jefferson Davis to discuss peace. On January 12 Blair met Davis, who gave him a letter expressing his willingness to send or receive a commission "with a view to secure peace to the two countries." Blair returned to Washington and showed the letter to Lincoln, who, on January 18, responded with one in which he expressed his willingness to receive any agent Davis "may informally send to me with the view of securing peace to the people of our one common country." A few days later, Blair showed Davis Lincoln's letter.[6]

On January 29 a peace commission dispatched by Davis, consisting of Confederate vice president Alexander Stephens, Senator Robert M. T. Hunter of Virginia, and former associate justice of the U.S. Supreme Court John A. Campbell, tried to enter the Union lines. The next day, Lincoln drafted orders for Major Thomas T. Eckert to meet with the party. According to a letter to be delivered to the commissioners, they could pass through the Union lines to go to Fort Monroe for an "informal conferrence [*sic*]" if they agreed to the terms of Lincoln's letter dated January 18, 1865. Lincoln wished to make clear that any negotiation needed to be based on reunion—not the "two countries" mentioned in Davis's letter but the "one common country" referenced in his.[7]

On the morning of January 31, Lincoln received a telegram from General Grant that he had already given instructions for the party to cross through the Union lines and that he expected them at his headquarters at City Point, Virginia, that evening. At 1:30 P.M., while the House deliberated on the amendment, Lincoln responded by return telegram to alert Grant that Eckert would arrive with instructions. Lincoln told Grant to act upon the message "as far as applicable," now that the general had allowed the party through the lines. Lincoln also penned instructions to Secretary of State Seward to proceed to Fort Monroe, "there to meet, and informally confer with Messrs. Stephens, Hunter, and Campbell." Lincoln ordered Seward to "make known to them that three things are indispensable":

1. The restoration of the national authority throughout all the States.
2. No receding, by the Executive of the United States on the Slavery question, from the position assumed thereon, in the late Annual Message to Congress, and in preceding documents.
3. No cessation of hostilities short of an end of the war, and the disbanding of all forces hostile to the government.

Otherwise, Lincoln instructed Seward, "inform them that all propositions of theirs not inconsistent with the above, will be considered and passed upon in a spirit of sincere liberality," adding that his secretary of state "will not assume to definitely consummate anything."[8]

After the war, Ashley admitted that Lincoln knew about these developments when he wrote the letter to appease Cox, adding, "You see how admirably he answered my note for my purposes and yet how *truly*." Lincoln also confessed the matter to abolitionist Elizabeth Peabody, sister to the wives of Nathaniel Hawthorne and Horace Mann, who twice met with Lincoln in February 1865. In writing about the first meeting, Peabody commented on Lincoln's "mobile countenance" and how he gave the "sweetest smile" even when mentioning one of his loudest critics, Wendell Phillips. When Peabody brought up the amendment, Lincoln "looked up suddenly & eagerly & very brightly and said—'What do you think I was doing that day?

I was writing my instructions to Seward!!'" According to Peabody, Lincoln then recounted the story behind the communication with Ashley: "There is a little secret piece of history connected with that. I had dismissed—some time before—all anxiety about that voting. *I knew the bill would pass*—the day he introduced it—But you know Ashley wanted to get a larger majority & so put off putting the *question* for a fortnight—and meantime that Peace Commissioner business *came on*—You look at the date of that correspondence. I *eased it along* and concluded to send Seward down[.] Twice—while the talk in Congress was going on that morning—& I was writing to Seward—notes came from the House asking me *if there were any Commissioners of Peace in Washington*—or *whether I thought they would come*. Those converts of Ashley's would have gone off in a tangent at the last moment had they smelt Peace. I left off writing each time—& took sheets of paper—& elaborately wrote that '*as far as I knew* there were no Commissioners of peace in Washington—*nor did I think they would come!*' Here he laughed—& repeated again in the same words & with the same emphasis '*as far as I knew &c.*'"[9]

Finally, shortly after 3:00 P.M. on January 31, the time for voting had come. Several Supreme Court justices, various senators, Secretary of the Treasury William Pitt Fessenden, and Montgomery Blair and his successor as postmaster general, William Dennison, attended. In the packed galleries, reporters, abolitionist women, and African Americans, including Frederick Douglass's son Charles, waited.[10]

During the roll call, eleven representatives who had voted against the measure in June 1864 now voted for it. While the Speaker of the House typically did not vote, Schuyler Colfax asked the clerk to call his name so that it, too, could be recorded in favor of the amendment. Jubilation ensued when the resolution passed with two votes to spare on a vote of 119 to 56, with eight absent: representatives threw hats in the air, shouting and applause ringed the chamber from both the floor and the gallery, some people hugged, and women waved handkerchiefs. One black man who did not want to celebrate in public went to a vacant room and danced by himself. The House adjourned and word immediately spread across the country, generating rallies. At 4:15 P.M., the War Department received a telegram to Lincoln from

John G. Nicolay that simply read, "Constitutional amendment just passed by 119 for to 56 votes against."[11]

Ten lame-duck Democrats voted in favor of the amendment, along with Alexander Coffroth of Pennsylvania and Augustus C. Baldwin of Michigan (both of whose reelections were contested), William Radford of New York (who had been reelected), and John A. Griswold of New York (who had been elected to the Thirty-Eighth Congress as a Democrat but won reelection as a Republican). Of the eight members who did not vote, all were Democrats, five were lame ducks, Francis Le Blond of Ohio and Andrew Jackson Rogers of New Jersey had been reelected, and Daniel Voorhees was in Indiana due to a family illness. Of the Border State delegations, all the representatives from Maryland (four) and Delaware (one) voted in favor, as did seven of Missouri's representatives (two voted against) and four of Kentucky's (five voted against).[12]

On one hand, the vote provides an indication of the level of party fluidity as of early 1865, but it almost immediately gave rise to rumors that corruption had aided the resolution's passage. As early as January 9, Representative Robert Mallory of Kentucky, who voted against the amendment, charged the possibility of Republican favors in exchange for votes, and he explicitly linked Lincoln to it: "The wish or order of the President is very potent. He can punish and reward." While Mallory did not point to anything specific—in fact, he said the only "potent influence" he saw at the time of his speech was Lincoln's request in his Annual Message—Mallory's implication was clear. Long after passage, two Republican representatives made statements in their memoirs indicating backroom dealings. George S. Boutwell of Massachusetts recalled in 1902, "Mr. Ashley was deeply interested in the passage of the resolution and it was believed that he made pledges which no one but the President could keep. Such was the exigency for the passage of the resolution that the means were not subjected to any rigid rule of ethics." George W. Julian of Indiana, meanwhile, wrote in 1884 that passage of the resolution "depended upon certain negotiations, the result of which was not fully assured, and the particulars of which never reached the public."[13]

Yet, no credible evidence indicates any actual bribe taken by anyone voting in favor of the amendment. Members of the Seward lobby implied in letters the availability of bribe money, and William N. Bilbo's letter to Andrew Johnson dated January 10 all but says such money was given ("*material* arguments"), though no conclusive evidence has surfaced. On February 13, 1865, Richard Schell wrote to Seward's son that "a Gentleman called today to have me give an acct of expenses to Washington. Which amt to nothing at any time that I can be of any service to the Hon Sec of state or yourself I will do all I can but at my own expence [*sic*]." Schell's letter implies that Seward or his office planned to reimburse for expenditures related to the lobbying efforts, though Schell's letter remains unclear as to what those expenses included.[14]

"Sunset" Cox in 1885 recalled that he boarded with a Republican who, upon learning of his vote against the amendment, "broke forth into such a torrent of abuse." According to Cox, the unnamed individual exclaimed that certain New York parties had promised him $10,000 from a fund "to be ready and freely used for corrupting members" in exchange for convincing Cox to vote in favor. Cox called it "monstrous" that the effort to "amend the Constitution upon such a humane and glorious theme" involved "the aid of the lucre of office-holders," but his story seems fictional. Cox did not mention the incident in his 1865 memoir, nor did he reference any type of corruption at all surrounding the Thirteenth Amendment's passage in that volume. Instead, the story appeared in his 1885 memoir, at a time when Cox had regained a congressional seat by campaigning on the issue of Republican financial misdeeds, and in his account he emphasized the Republican identity of the purported briber. Moreover, Cox already had indicated his likelihood to support the amendment and even quietly lobbied on behalf of its passage. Cox voted against the measure at the last minute because he feared it would derail peace talks on the basis of an institution, slavery, that he thought to be dead anyway as a consequence of the war.[15]

Republican representative John B. Alley of Massachusetts in the mid-1880s recalled that at a certain point in January, it seemed the tally would be two votes shy of success when Lincoln summoned two congressmen (it is not clear whether Alley was one of them) and told them to procure the necessary votes. When the two representatives asked Lincoln how to do so, Alley had him saying, "I am President of the United States, clothed with great power. The abolition of slavery by constitutional provision settles the fate, for all coming time, not only of the millions now in bondage, but of unborn millions to come—a measure of such importance that those two votes must be procured. I leave it to you to determine how it shall be done; but remember that I am President of the United States, clothed with immense power, and I expect you to procure those votes." Besides the fact that Lincoln likely never would have been so indiscreet in implying promises in exchange for votes, the entire exchange seems overly dramatic and out of character. It is hard to imagine Lincoln thundering an almost-threatening statement such as this one. Moreover, the same collection of reminiscences about Lincoln in which Alley's account appears includes one from Schuyler Colfax, who said of Lincoln's use of pardons, "No man clothed with such vast power ever wielded it more tenderly and more forbearingly." Thus, one can see an almost verbatim use of the motif given in Alley's account.[16]

Charles A. Dana, who served as assistant secretary of war in 1864–65, claimed decades later that Lincoln rushed Nevada's admission to statehood so as to help ratify the Thirteenth Amendment. According to Dana, the vote for enabling Nevada to form a state government came up in the House in March 1864, and Lincoln told him, "Dana, I am very anxious about this vote. It has got to be taken next week. The time is very short. It is going to be a great deal closer than I wish it was." According to Dana, Lincoln then identified a congressman from New Jersey and two from New York and suggested they were men "you can deal with better than anybody else, perhaps, as you know them all." To Dana's query as to what they would likely want, he had Lincoln replying, "I don't know. It makes no difference, though, what they want. Here is the alternative: that we carry this vote, or be compelled to raise another million, and I don't know how many more, men, and fight no one knows how long. It is a question of three votes or new armies." Dana also recounted Lincoln saying, "Whatever promise you make to them I will perform."[17]

According to Dana, two of the congressmen wanted internal revenue collector's appointments while the third wanted to control an appointment at the New York Custom House. Dana assured all of them they would receive their request, and consequently they voted that Nevada be allowed to form a state government. Nevada ratified the Thirteenth Amendment the following February, and in Dana's view, "this little piece of side politics was one of the most judicious, humane, and wise uses of executive authority that I have ever assisted in or witnessed." Dana added that Lincoln's assassination meant the custom house appointment was never made.[18]

Numerous problems plague Dana's account, which confuses the effort in Congress in January 1865 to pass the amendment resolution. Lincoln was not thinking about ratification of the as-yet unpassed Thirteenth Amendment in March 1864. In fact, Lincoln had not even endorsed the amendment at this point. Moreover, Congress approved the act to enable Nevada to begin the process of becoming a state with little dissent. While Lincoln welcomed Nevada for its additional votes in Congress, he did not seem to be in much of a hurry to proclaim it a state in time to gain its electoral votes in 1864, doing so only days before the election.[19]

On the other hand, Dana's story has a kernel of truth to it regarding the one appointment Lincoln may have made as a favor. The appointment does not seem to have been a quid pro quo arrangement, however, in that it involved Representative Anson Herrick of New York, a one-term Democrat who published the weekly *New York Atlas*. Herrick favored the amendment ideologically—his paper even published editorials in its favor, and he delivered a speech in support of the amendment on the day of the final vote. More likely, Herrick was an opportunist who saw a way to capitalize on his vote so as to help a family member.[20]

In mid-June, Montgomery Blair identified Herrick by name as a man "whose vote was paid for by an apt." In July 1865, Herrick wrote Seward that they had never met but Homer A. Nelson had given "assurances" of Seward's "friendship . . . in appreciation" for his "breaking from the ties of party and casting my lot with the few democratic members who resolved to 'eat no more dirt' in the cause of human Slavery." Herrick reported that Lincoln, "at the instance of the friends of his administration" who managed the amendment, had nominated his brother Hugh M. Herrick for the position of internal revenue assessor for the district Herrick represented in Congress. The Senate referred the appointment to the finance committee, and according to Herrick, Lincoln "after the adjournment signified to me and my friends that he considered himself in honor bound to consummate that appointment, but at the request of Senator [Ira] Harris [of New York], whose personal friend was to have been removed to give place to Herrick, he consented to let the matter stand over for a few days, *not to exceed a month*, to give the Senator opportunity to provide some other office for his friend." Lincoln had, on March 9, 1865, nominated Hugh M. Herrick to be assessor of internal revenue for a district in New York, in place of Homer Franklin, who had already been removed.[21]

Lincoln's assassination intervened, and Herrick in July 1865 wrote Secretary of State Seward that President Johnson told Charles Dana he would make the appointment if Secretary of the Treasury Hugh McCulloch recommended it. According to Herrick, McCulloch worried that "somebody will charge 'bargain and corruption' upon Abraham Lincoln and myself, to the shame and disgrace of the present administration, if so marked a favor should be extended to a Constitutional Amendment democrat of the House of Representatives, as the appointment of his brother to a paltry office in his district, albeit that brother has been an active republican partisan." Herrick asked for the matter to be "adjusted in accordance with the principles of honor and good faith" and the "memory of President Lincoln."[22]

Herrick grew more strident when his letter failed to get the desired result. In August 1865 he wrote Seward that he had conferred with Homer A. Nelson, "who last winter proposed to have authority to pledge *your faith* in the matter" and who had cooperated with Ashley, Dana, Representative Augustus Frank, and former Representative Abram Wakeman "in their efforts to bring me 'from darkness to light.'" Herrick asked if all of these individuals were "'Confidence Men,'" and continued, "President Lincoln told me in person that whatever Ashley had promised should be performed, and he signified his good faith by sending the name to the Senate; and had he lived I probably would not have been subjected to the humiliation I have encountered in this matter." Nelson also wrote Seward that Ashley and Frank had agreed upon the appointment, adding, "For reasons which you probably recall *I pledged my word*" that the appointment would be made. Herrick's effort on behalf of his brother came to naught, but in February 1867 he wrote Seward seeking for himself the position of collector of internal revenue in his old district. Herrick asked Seward not to refer the letter to the secretary of the Treasury, and Seward took the opportunity to respond, simply, "I can properly receive no *private* letters concerning Treasury Department that I am not to refer to the head of that Department." Herrick died the following February and, with him, so did this matter.[23]

Historians have inaccurately identified appointments for lame-duck Democrats George H. Yeaman and Moses F. Odell as quid pro quo actions for their votes on the amendment. It was President Johnson, not Lincoln, who nominated Yeaman to be minister to Denmark in December 1865, and Johnson had given Odell a commission for naval agent for the port of New York during the Senate recess and renominated him once the Senate was back in session. The Senate confirmed both appointments. Odell had joined three other Democrats to vote for the amendment in June 1864. Homer Nelson declined the offer of a position abroad and later asked Seward's help in obtaining a position in the Treasury Department. Of the Democrats who voted in favor of the amendment or did not vote, no substantive correspondence to Lincoln exists in his papers at the Library of Congress, nor does the *Senate Executive Journal* list any relevant appointments by him. The only thing that comes close is Hugh M. Herrick, and even there, no direct link to Lincoln exists. Other individuals seem to have made the promise to Herrick's brother, and Lincoln honored their request.[24]

Lincoln explicitly declined to get involved in another effort to secure votes for the amendment resolution. This matter involved the Camden and Amboy Railroad, which had been granted by the state a monopoly on traffic in central New Jersey, something that complicated civilian passenger travel and Union troop movements alike. When the War Department sought to use the nearby Raritan and Delaware Bay Railroad, the Camden and Amboy sued in state court, which in February 1864 required that all traffic between the two cities be hauled on its line. Republicans proposed legislation to authorize use of the other line, and on January 16, 1865, the Senate began debating a bill that proposed, "Every railroad company in the United States whose road is operated by steam . . . shall be authorized to carry upon and over its road . . . all freight, property, mails, passengers, troops, and Government supplies on their way from any State to another State, and to receive compensation therefor." As the bill relied on the Constitution's Commerce Clause, the debate about it delved into the boundaries of federal authority under that provision as well as into the New Jersey situation in particular. In the Senate, Charles Sumner championed the bill, declaring the matter a decision between "public convenience and the Union itself in its beneficent powers on the one side. Public inconvenience and all the discord of intolerable State pretensions on the other side." In response, the Camden and Amboy mobilized its lobbyists to try to block the action, who proposed to Ashley that they could help the cause of the amendment if he could convince Sumner to back off.[25]

Lincoln's secretary John Nicolay wrote that on January 18, he went to Lincoln at Ashley's request because "the Camden and Amboy Railroad interest promised Mr. Ashley that if he would help postpone the Raritan railroad bill over this session they would in return make the New Jersey Democrats help about the amendment, either by their votes or absence. Sumner being the Senate champion of the Raritan bill, Ashley went to him to ask him to drop it for this session. Sumner, however, showed reluctance to adopt Mr. Ashley's suggestion, saying that he hoped the amendment would pass anyhow, etc." Ashley provided Nicolay with two reasons for Sumner's intransigence: he had his own version of an amendment that he hoped would be adopted if the current one went down to defeat, and "Sumner thinks the defeat of the Camden and Amboy monopoly would establish a principle by legislative enactment which would effectually crush out the last lingering relics of the States rights dogma."[26]

Ashley thus hoped Lincoln would "urge" Sumner "to be practical and secure the passage of the amendment in the manner suggested," but when Nicolay brought up the matter, Lincoln replied, "I can do nothing with Mr. Sumner in these matters. While Mr. Sumner is very cordial with me, he is making his history in an issue with me on this very point. He hopes to succeed in beating the President so as to change this Government from its original form and make it a strong centralized power." Calling Ashley into the room, Lincoln said, "I think I understand Mr. Sumner; and I think he would be all the more resolute in his persistence on the points which Mr. Nicolay has mentioned to me if he supposed I were at all watching his course on this matter."[27]

Decades after the vote, Representative George S. Boutwell of Massachusetts recalled a rumor that Ashley made "arrangements with certain Democrats to absent themselves from the House when the vote was taken." Albert G. Riddle, meanwhile, who had represented Ohio in the prior Congress and did not serve in 1865, recalled in 1893, "It was found necessary to secure the absence of one Democrat from the House on the day of the vote. A railroad in Pennsylvania was threatened with the passage of a bill by Congress greatly adverse to its interests—the bill was in Mr. Sumner's hands, ready to be reported; the road had struggled to have action on the bill deferred till the next Congress—thus far without avail. The lawyer for the railroad was a Democratic member of the present House." According to Riddle's account, "the railroad's lawyer was taken so ill that he could not be carried to the House . . . and the august Sumner did not report the bill during that session."[28]

Despite some factual errors in Riddle's account, it does seem Ashley struck a deal without Lincoln's help, or at least dangled the implication of one, with the railroad's lobby on the proposed Thirteenth Amendment. In the alternative, perhaps the railroad's lobbyists made a deal with some senators. In any event, two of the Democrats representing New Jersey in the House did not vote, and one of them was an agent of the Camden and Amboy Railroad, Andrew Jackson Rogers. While the other representative, George Middleton, had a poor voting record on contentious legislation, Rogers earlier had been outspoken in his opposition to the amendment. He had delivered a speech claiming that decisions about slavery belonged to the jurisdiction of individual states and thus it was beyond the power of the people to interfere with them by amendment. Circumstantial evidence supporting the likelihood of a deal comes in the fact that Missouri's James S. Rollins announced to the House Rogers's absence due to illness on the day of the final vote.[29]

The antimonopoly bill stalled in the Senate, and the implication of corruption percolated. On February 23 Democratic senator Willard Saulsbury of Delaware referenced "lobby agents" that had come into the Senate to try to control its activities, and he asked, "I want to know whether there is any political intrigue, whether the Democratic party of this country is sold by the Camden and Amboy Railroad Company or not." While historian William Gillette calls the evidence "inconclusive" as to whether a deal was struck with Rogers, the fact that the New Jersey legislature later declined to ratify the Thirteenth Amendment suggests that any such deal ended with him. As for the Camden and Amboy, it merged in 1867 with the New Jersey Railroad to form the United New Jersey Railways and Canal Company, and the monopoly that it carried into that relationship expired in 1869.[30]

James M. Scovel, who served in the New Jersey state legislature during the Civil War and hated the Camden and Amboy, in 1898 wrote a brief article about Representative Thaddeus Stevens of Pennsylvania, who supported Scovel's aspirations to serve in Congress. According to Scovel, "influence from the White House secured votes against a favorite measure of Mr. Stevens for an air-line railway from Washington to New York and . . . these same votes helped Mr. Lincoln's great amendment for emancipation." Scovel also had Stevens, who died decades earlier, say, without any corroboration, "'The greatest measure of the nineteenth century was passed by corruption, aided and abetted by the purest man in America.'" If Scovel meant to refer to the Camden and Amboy Railroad situation, however, it is important to remember that Lincoln explicitly rejected Ashley's request to intervene.[31]

Another possible deal, which again did not include Lincoln, involved the vote of Alexander Coffroth of Pennsylvania, a Democrat whose reelection was contested. Former representative Albert G. Riddle wrote of a contested seat involving a Democrat who "came to see that the result would depend entirely upon his vote on the impending 13th amendment" and who accordingly "secured his seat in the 39th

Congress." Coffroth did change his June 1864 vote, but in a speech he delivered on the day of the final vote, he affirmed his allegiance to the Democratic Party and explained that he acted to remove the slavery issue from politics, especially because it had brought the Republicans to power. Moreover, Coffroth had a strong friendship with Lincoln and later served as one of the president's pallbearers. That fact, coupled with his speech, makes it seem more likely that Coffroth had made a genuine conversion, though he no doubt hoped his vote would help him retain his seat. Coffroth received his seat in the next Congress, but he ultimately lost it when his challenger continued to contest the election. Another Democrat who voted in favor of the amendment, Augustus C. Baldwin of Michigan, unsuccessfully contested his election as well.[32]

Allegations that Lincoln involved himself directly in inappropriate measures collapse under closer scrutiny, and he seems to have relied on moral and political suasion in trying to support the amendment. The only matter in which Lincoln appears to have been directly involved was an appointment for Representative Anson Herrick's brother. The passage of the amendment did involve a lot of backroom negotiation, however, and included a variety of people ranging from Representatives James M. Ashley of Ohio and James S. Rollins of Missouri, members of the Seward lobby, and Montgomery Blair to even some Democrats such as "Sunset" Cox. Whatever the tenor of those discussions, Lincoln seems to have steered clear of any personal unsavoriness, though he likely knew about most of the politicking taking place in an effort to have the Thirty-Eighth Congress pass the amendment resolution before it adjourned in March.

CHAPTER EIGHT

PEACE, RATIFICATION, AND THE THIRTEENTH AMENDMENT

A busy day awaited Lincoln when he awoke on February 1, 1865. The president monitored developments concerning the Confederate peace commissioners and sent a telegram to General Grant at 9:30 A.M.: "Let nothing which is transpiring, change, hinder, or delay your Military movements, or plans." At 5:30 P.M. the president also telegraphed instructions to Major Eckert.[1]

In between sending these telegrams, Lincoln endorsed the official copy of the resolution submitting the amendment to the states, signing it along with the words, "Approved, February 1. 1865." Lincoln would sign in total twelve souvenir copies of this amendment resolution as well, all on large folio vellum leaves and ranging in number of additional signers from 2 to more than 160, including senators and representatives. Secretary of State Seward had ordered that certified copies of the amendment be sent to every state governor that same day.[2]

Massachusetts governor John A. Andrew, who had practiced law, assumed that a presidential signature was necessary to make the resolution valid. The War Department Telegraph Office received a telegram that morning from Andrew requesting from Lincoln a return message "so that I may know as nearly as possible the moment you will sign the resolution for amending the Constitution," adding that he wished to "echo it immediately by a National Salute on Boston Common, with a chorus of all the Church bells of Massachusetts."[3]

A presidential signature, however, is not necessary on a resolution to amend the Constitution. Lincoln's signing irked some members of Congress as an unconstitutional expansion of executive power. On February 4, Senator Lyman Trumbull of Illinois moved a resolution that the amendment had been "inadvertently presented to the President for his approval" and to declare "such approval was unnecessary to give effect to the action of Congress in proposing said amendment . . . and being inadvertently done, should not constitute a precedent for the future." After a brief debate, in which Trumbull cited a 1798 Supreme Court case that held the president "has nothing to do with the proposition, or adoption, of amendments to the Constitution," the Senate approved the resolution on February 7, 1865.[4]

Former Massachusetts congressman John Z. Goodrich, now serving as collector of the port of Boston, understood why Lincoln signed the amendment. Goodrich wrote Lincoln to congratulate him on having the "privilege" of signing an amendment "which is soon not only to free every slave in the land, not freed before, but to eradicate utterly & from every vestige of the slave system, or the power to enslave." Goodrich remarked that doing so "must have done much to compensate" Lincoln for his "labor & anxiety" since he assumed office and, noting the amendment's passage before the end of his first term, observed, "It is alone proof of astounding progress, such as no one could have predicted or believed at its commencement." Separately, Lincoln likely felt it better to act out of an abundance of caution—Governor Andrew thought the resolution required a presidential signature, for instance—and there was no harm in eliminating any possible technical problem with such an easy solution.[5]

By 7:25 P.M. on February 1, a telegram arrived for Lincoln from Governor Richard J. Oglesby indicating that Illinois' legislature had ratified the amendment. Oglesby added, "All suppose you had signed the Joint resolution of Congress." Five minutes later, another telegram arrived from Ward H. Lamon and Edward L. Baker in Illinois indicating the same news, reporting it had been done "with a great hurrah."[6]

Lincoln then responded to a throng of celebrants outside the White House, calling the occasion "one of congratulation to the country and to the whole world" but reminding them, "There is a task yet before us—to go forward and consummate by the votes of the States that which Congress so nobly began yesterday." Lincoln announced that he "had the honor to inform those present that Illinois had already to-day done the work" and that "Maryland was about half through; but he felt proud that Illinois was a little ahead." Lincoln cast the amendment as important both for its moral implications and for helping build a stronger nation-state; he "wished the reunion of all the States perfected and so effected as to remove all causes of disturbance in the future; and to attain this end it was necessary that the original disturbing cause should, if possible, be rooted out." Moreover, Lincoln "thought all would bear him witness that he had never shrunk from doing all that he could to eradicate Slavery

Lincoln opening an envelope of broken chains with the passage of the Thirteenth Amendment. "Uncle Abe's Valentine Sent by Columbia" in *Frank Leslie's Illustrated Newspaper*, February 1865. Library of Congress.

by issuing an emancipation proclamation." While acknowledging "that proclamation falls far short of what the amendment will be when fully consummated," Lincoln wanted to remind everyone of his antislavery credentials and that he had helped prepare the way for the amendment. Lincoln acknowledged that some people might question the legal validity and operation of the proclamation and say "it did not meet the evil. But this amendment is a King's cure for all the evils." Lincoln ended by congratulating all present, the country, and the world "upon this great moral victory."[7]

Also occupying Lincoln's mind was the peace mission in Virginia, which seemed to be sputtering. Eckert had met with the commissioners, and it seemed to him they had rejected the "one country" approach outlined in Lincoln's January 18 letter. Eckert notified the president, who had prepared to recall Seward from Fort Monroe. The Confederate commissioners, however, without President Jefferson Davis's approval, then wrote Grant that they accepted the conditions of that letter and still wished to confer. Late that night, Grant sent a telegram to Lincoln, who received it early the next morning, and assured the president, "I am convinced, upon conversation with Messrs Stevens [*sic*] & Hunter that their intentions are good and their desire sincere to restore peace and union." Lincoln, excited by Grant's assessment and the prospect of ending the war, the next morning communicated to Grant and Seward that he would go to Fort Monroe in person as soon as possible. Shortly afterward, Lincoln departed Washington for the conference.[8]

Lincoln arrived at nearby Hampton Roads, Virginia, on the night of February 2, and the next morning he and Seward met with Alexander Stephens, Robert M. T. Hunter, and John A. Campbell aboard a steamer. As Lincoln later reported to Congress, "The whole substance of the instructions to the Secretary of State . . . was stated and insisted upon, and nothing was said inconsistently therewith," but the "conferrence [*sic*] ended without result."[9]

The Confederate commissioners recalled matters a little differently, and the Thirteenth Amendment features prominently in their accounts. Stephens wrote a few years later that Seward told the commissioners that Congress had passed the amendment and, casting it as a war measure, implied that the Confederate states could probably block the measure from ratification if they returned to the Union. According to a memorandum drafted by Campbell shortly after the conference, Seward identified the amendment as a war measure and said that if the war ended, issues relating to the war probably would be abandoned. Years later, Campbell recalled Seward saying, "The Southern States will return to the Union, and with their own strength and the aid of the connections they will form with other States, this amendment will be defeated."[10]

It seems incredibly unlikely that Seward would have discussed, or Lincoln tolerated, defeat for the amendment they had worked so hard to bring about, especially when much of the urgency came from Lincoln's desire to say the matter was out of his hands in the event of any negotiation. Moreover, Lincoln reported to the House that the instructions to Seward were "stated and insisted upon." The second point of those instructions explicitly held that the executive would not recede from the position he had announced in his last message to Congress, in which he called for adoption of the amendment resolution. While Lincoln and Seward did insist on inclusion of the Confederate states in the ratification process, it seems the accuracy of Stephens's and Campbell's accounts end there on this point.[11]

Stephens also recalled Lincoln expressing apprehension about the turmoil that immediate emancipation might create. This statement comports with Lincoln's long-held concern about the issue, most often manifested in his support for gradual emancipation schemes. Stephens, however, then had Lincoln say something that is almost certainly inaccurate. According to the Confederate vice president, after a moment of quiet reflection, Lincoln said, "Stephens, if I were in Georgia, and entertained the sentiments I do—though, I suppose, I should not be permitted to stay there long with them; but if I resided in Georgia, with my present sentiments, I'll tell you what I would do, if I were in your place: I would go home and get the Governor of the State to call the Legislature together, and get them to recall all the State troops from the war; elect Senators and Members to Congress, and ratify this Constitutional Amendment *prospectively*, so as to take effect—say in five years. Such a ratification would be valid in my opinion. I have looked into the subject, and think such a prospective ratification would be valid." Lincoln continued by advising Stephens, "Whatever may have been the views of your people before the war, they must be convinced now, that Slavery is doomed. It cannot last long in any event, and the best course, it seems to me, for your public men to pursue, would be to adopt such a policy as will avoid, as far as possible, the evils of immediate emancipation. This would be my course, if I were in your place."[12]

It is nearly impossible to believe the careful constitutional thinker in Lincoln would have made this proposal. Article V of the Constitution does not preclude the idea of prospective ratification, but it does not authorize it, either. Critically, the text of the proposed amendment did not provide for prospective ratification. Moreover, even if Lincoln accepted the concept, he must have realized the unlikelihood that Congress or the Supreme Court would do so.

Stephens also recounted Lincoln as saying that "he would be willing to be taxed to remunerate the Southern people for their slaves" and that he "believed the people of the North were as responsible for slavery as the people of the South, and if the war should then cease, with the voluntary abolition of slavery by the States, he should be in favor, individually, of the Government paying a fair indemnity for the loss to the owners." According to Stephens, Lincoln intimated that he "knew some who were in favor of an appropriation as high as Four Hundred Millions of Dollars for this purpose. . . . But on this subject he said he could give no assurance—enter into no stipulation." Campbell in February 1865 recorded substantially the same point: "Mr. Seward at one time said, that the Northern States were weary of war, and would be willing to pay what they would probably be required to pay on account of its continuance, but did not explain himself further on this subject. Mr. Lincoln stated that he regarded the North to be as much responsible for slavery as the South, and that he would be rejoiced to be taxed on his little property for indemnities to the masters of slaves. Mr. Seward remarked that the North had already paid on that account." These statements are close in keeping with views Lincoln expressed to his cabinet a few days later as well as in his Second Inaugural Address.[13]

In their report to Jefferson Davis about the conference, the commissioners mentioned that Lincoln and Seward had brought the proposed amendment to their notice. Days after the conference, Davis reported to his Congress that Lincoln had told the commissioners about the amendment to make clear "the question of slavery was wholly removed from his control and placed beyond negotiation." In Richmond the conference was seen as example of Northern obstinacy, and on February 9 Hunter delivered a speech in Richmond criticizing Lincoln, defending slavery, and warning that Union victory would mean freedom for slaves.[14]

In the North, people heard speeches of a different tenor. On February 4, 1865, William Lloyd Garrison spoke in praise of Lincoln at Boston's Music Hall: "And to whom is the country more immediately indebted for this vital and saving amendment of the Constitution than, perhaps, to any other man? I believe I may confidently answer—to the humble railsplitter of Illinois—to the Presidential chainbreaker for millions of the oppressed—to Abraham Lincoln!" After the audience delivered applause and three cheers for Lincoln, Garrison continued, "I understand that it was by his wish and influence that that plank was made a part of the Baltimore platform; and taking his position unflinchingly upon that platform, the people have overwhelmingly sustained both him and it, in ushering in the year of jubilee."[15]

Lincoln got concerned on February 5 when Kentucky governor Thomas E. Bramlette telegraphed him that he had not yet received the official copy of the amendment. "Will send official copy of Constitutional amendment by mail to-morrow, this being Sunday," Lincoln telegraphed back, adding, "Precedents justify the Legislature to act on *ex-officio* notice, of congress having passed the proposed amendment; nevertheless I will send you the authenticated copy." Lincoln must have asked Seward about the matter because his secretary of state replied that same day, "A certified copy of Constitutional Amendment was sent (as I had directed) to every Governor of every state on Wednesday last. Bramlette included. He will be so advised by telegraph to day."[16]

That same day, Lincoln made an unpopular proposal, one that indicated he still held onto the idea of compensated emancipation and corroborates that portion of Stephens's account of the Hampton Roads conference. On February 5, 1865, Lincoln met with the cabinet to discuss a joint resolution he planned to present to Congress and that resurrected the substance, if not the form, of the first amendment he had proposed in his Annual Message of 1862: "That the President of the United States is hereby empowered, in his discretion, to pay four hundred millions of dollars to [all slaveholding states, whether they had seceded or not] in the manner, and on the conditions following, towit [*sic*]: The payment to be made in six per cent government bonds, and to be distributed among said States pro rata on their respective slave populations, as shown by the census of 1860; and no part of said sum to be paid unless all resistance to the national authority shall be abandoned and cease, on or before the first day of April next; and upon such abandonment and ceasing of resistance, one half of said sum to be paid in manner aforesaid, and the remaining half to be paid only upon the amendment of the national constitution recently proposed by congress, becoming valid law, on or before the first day of July next, by the action thereon of the requisite number of States." Lincoln expressed his intention that, if the above conditions were met, "all political offences will be pardoned," "all property, except slaves, liable to confiscation or forfeiture, will be released therefrom, except in cases of intervening interests of third parties," and he would recommend to Congress that it act with "liberality . . . upon all points not lying within executive control."[17]

The cabinet rejected Lincoln's plan unanimously, and years later Secretary of the Interior John P. Usher recalled that Lincoln seemed "surprised." According to Usher, the president asked how long the war would last, and then, after a period of silence, Lincoln answered his own question: "A hundred days. We are spending now in carrying on the war $3,000,000 a day, which will amount to all this money, besides all the lives." Lincoln then added, "But you are all opposed to me and I will not send the message," and shortly after the meeting Lincoln wrote on his proposal, "To-day these papers, which explain themselves, were drawn up and submitted to the Cabinet & unanamously [*sic*] disapproved by them." The next day, Secretary of the Navy Gideon Welles recorded in his diary that "the earnest desire of the President to conciliate and effect peace was manifest, but there may be such a thing as so overdoing as to cause a distrust or adverse feeling. In the present temper of Congress the proposed measure, if a wise one, could not be carried through successfully; I do not think the scheme could accomplish any good results. The rebels would misconstrue it if the offer were made. If attempted and defeated it would do harm."[18]

Lincoln felt in better spirits during a White House reception a few days later. After Elizabeth Peabody observed the president's kind behavior with some young boys, she asked him if he had seen the issue of the *Liberator* in which Garrison's Music Hall speech appeared. After he replied that he had not, Peabody told Lincoln about speeches given by Garrison and Frederick Douglass, and Lincoln asked her if she had a copy with her. Peabody did, but she cautioned Lincoln that the issue also contained a more critical speech from Wendell Phillips. "Oh *that* is no matter," said Lincoln. "Give it to me. *I like to read his sharp things*," and he "very eagerly took the paper & put it into his pocket."[19]

As Lincoln stated on February 1, getting the amendment resolution through Congress was only one step in the process of revising the Constitution; ratification by three-fourths of the states came next. On this point, Lincoln's work for state-based emancipation, as well as his lenient Reconstruction plan, bore fruit: by the time Congress submitted the amendment for ratification, four slave states—Arkansas, Louisiana, Maryland, and Missouri—had abolished slavery (as had West Virginia, carved from Virginia). Tennessee voters approved on Washington's Birthday, February 22, 1865, an amendment to that state's constitution, proposed in January, that abolished slavery there. Besides helping set the climate for the Thirteenth Amendment in the first place, that fact that five states went from slave to free helped the chances of ratification, and all of them, as well as West Virginia, ratified the amendment before Lincoln died (the last of these six, Arkansas, did so on April 14, 1865).

A wrinkle existed because Lincoln held that no state had ever left the Union, and thus the Confederate states needed to participate in the ratification process for it to be valid. Some Radical Republicans disagreed. While the Constitution mentions ratification "by the Legislatures of three fourths of the several States," it does not address purported secession or how to calculate the number when the validity of some state legislatures is in dispute.

On February 4, Charles Sumner moved a resolution that would have required for ratification approval by three-fourths of the states being represented in Congress; states without representation in Congress would not count in the equation for ratification. Senator James R. Doolittle of Wisconsin a couple of weeks later made the point that "nine tenths of all the people of this country" believed twenty-seven states were needed for ratification, not nineteen, but Sumner shook his head and said no, adding in a heated exchange between the two Republicans that it should be three-fourths of the "*de facto* States."[20]

Congress adjourned before addressing the issue, leaving Lincoln to set the policy. In his last speech, two days after Confederate general Robert E. Lee's surrender on April 9, Lincoln explicitly rejected Sumner's position. Lincoln announced that the question of whether the "seceded States, so called, are in the Union or out of it" was not a "material one," identifying it as a "pernicious abstraction" that served no purpose but that "of dividing our friends." Lincoln continued by admitting that "the seceded States, so called, are out of their proper practical relation with the Union; and that the sole object of the government, civil and military, in regard to those States is to again get them into that proper practical relation." Lincoln said it was "easier, to do this, without deciding, or even considering, whether these states have even been out of the Union"—that, "finding themselves safely at home, it would be utterly immaterial whether they had ever been abroad."[21]

Lincoln next expressed some concern with the government that had been set up in Louisiana: he wished more people had been involved in the process and noted that the state had not given the franchise to black men. Lincoln now endorsed political rights for black men, announcing, "I would myself prefer that it were now conferred on the very intelligent, and on those who serve our cause as soldiers." John Wilkes Booth stood in the audience and told Lewis Paine and David Herold, "That means nigger citizenship," before promising, "That is the last speech he will ever make," and vowing, "By God, I'll put him through."[22]

Lincoln continued while his soon-to-be assassin muttered in rage to his co-conspirators, noting the benefit of bringing Louisiana back into the fold and improving its government rather than rejecting it. Moreover, concern about ratification helped guide his position. Lincoln noted that Louisiana's "legislature has already voted to ratify the constitutional amendment recently passed by Congress, abolishing slavery throughout the nation. These twelve thousand persons are thus fully committed to the Union, and to perpetual freedom in the state—committed to the very things, and nearly all the things the nation wants—and they ask the nation[']s recognition, and it's [*sic*] assistance to make good their committal." The president announced, "If we reject Louisiana, we also reject one vote in favor of the proposed amendment to the national constitution. To meet this proposition, it has been argued that no more than three fourths of those States which have not attempted secession are necessary to validly ratify the amendment. I do not commit myself against this, further than to say that such a ratification would be questionable, and sure to be persistently questioned; while a ratification by three fourths of all the States would be unquestioned and unquestionable."[23]

Lincoln thus affirmed that ratification meant three-fourths of all the states, including Confederate ones. He remained consistent in arguing that if the states never left the Union, they had to count in ratification, notwithstanding the "state suicide" and "conquered territory" theories of Senator Charles Sumner and Representative Thaddeus Stevens. Moreover, including the Confederate states comported with his overall plan to try to restore them to normal relations within the Union as quickly as possible. Lincoln also likely hoped that participating in ratification would help make it less difficult for some Southern white people to accept the end of slavery, especially as the decision would be national in application and come not from a decree but from the voice of the people as expressed through the constitutional amendment process.

With Congress out of session as of March 3, Lincoln's administration controlled the process until the next Congress convened in December. Lincoln's administration accepted the ratifications of Virginia (by the Pierpont government) as well as the Louisiana, Tennessee, and Arkansas state governments as formed under his Proclamation of Amnesty and Reconstruction dated December 8, 1863, and his successor accepted the ratifications of other Confederate states. Georgia on December 6, 1865, became the twenty-seventh state to ratify, and on December 18, 1865, Seward proclaimed the amendment adopted. By contrast, when Congress convened earlier that month, it had refused to seat delegations from some of the states that ratified the amendment. Former attorney general Edward Bates noted the paradox that the Constitution was thus changed by the votes of states declared by Radical Republicans not to exist. "And so, it seems, they are not *States in the Union*, yet they can enact a constitution for the United States!" Bates observed, asking, "Are these men mad?" By 1872 both the Democratic and Republican platforms affirmed the validity of the Thirteenth, Fourteenth, and Fifteenth Amendments, rendering such discussion theoretical.[24]

Counting thirty-six states (twenty-five Union and eleven Confederate states, including West Virginia and Nevada admitted to the Union during Lincoln's presidency) meant that at least two Confederate states needed to ratify the amendment for it to go into effect, assuming all the Union ones did so. Not all the Union states did, however, making Lincoln's policy regarding the Confederate states all the more important for the amendment's ratification. Delaware rejected the amendment in February, and on March 2, Governor Thomas E. Bramlette of Kentucky reported that his state legislature had rejected the amendment despite his dissent. Bramlette assured Lincoln, "I believe the people of Kentucky will reverse this action of the Legislature; we shall see," and also informed the president that a proposal Bramlette had made to try to induce the state legislature to ratify—that Kentucky's ratification be contingent on receiving federal money to compensate slaveholders—had led some Kentuckians to charge the two of them with a "bargain."[25]

As slave states, non-ratification by Kentucky and Delaware does not seem surprising. New Jersey's rejection, however, appears a little more unexpected until one recognizes the strong Democratic Party in that state as well as that the lower half of free-state New Jersey faced slave-state Delaware across the Delaware River and Delaware Bay. An intense debate took place in the state legislature, with the Democrats who opposed ratification objecting to the means used, arguing that slavery was solely the purview of individual states, and raising fear about equality for black people. Lincoln figured prominently in some of the speeches.[26]

State assemblyman James C. Goble, who opposed amending the Constitution, argued, "When Abraham Lincoln came into power, he called the colored people niggers, then negroes, declaring that they were a different race, that they could not live with us, that they must colonize and go by themselves. In less than a year from that time, and ever since, they have by him and his party been styled 'American citizens of African descent,' while it appears to me that the negro tendency is still upward with the party in power." As to the argument that the people had endorsed the amendment in reelecting Lincoln, Goble announced, "New Jersey is exempted, and ought not be called upon to ratify; for she entered her solemn protest against Abraham Lincoln, his amendments, and all his policy, twice, in 1860 and 1864, and so will we, her legislators, record our protest against ratification . . . in this the noblest act of our lives."[27]

New Jersey state legislator Bernard Kearney likewise excoriated Lincoln, claiming, "The practice of violating this fundamental law of self-government has been and continues to be of frequent occurrence under our immaculate administration, of whom I desire to speak with caution and a certain degree of respect; especially His Excellency, 'Honest Old Abe,' our jocular national story-teller." Kearney noted the inconsistency with which Lincoln said in his First Inaugural that he would not interfere with slavery in states where it existed and "now 'rides the whirlwind and directs the storm.'" Kearney blamed the ministrations of "evil counsellors" who "distilled into his ears their poisonous and corrupting ideas and Honest Old Abe became their victim."[28]

New Jersey assemblyman Leon Abbett, who said he did not like slavery but wanted to see it abolished by state legislation, expressed his concern for state sovereignty, especially where the amendment meant "the loyal States of Delaware and Kentucky would be robbed of their property, under the color of law." Moreover, Abbett opposed the administration's policy on ratification: "I am unwilling to trust William H. Seward with such discretionary power. . . . He would count four 'sham' State governments, and declare the amendment adopted and the entire military power of the country would be used to enforce his decree. We all know that in this matter Mr. Seward would be the mere creature of the President."[29]

Legislator Charles C. Lathrop, however, called for New Jersey to join Maryland, West Virginia, Missouri, Louisiana, Tennessee, and Arkansas in "cutting loose from the polluting carcass." Having opposed Lincoln's election in 1860, Lathrop now stated, "I believe that in the Providence of God a man has been brought to the executive chair though in opposition to my vote on his first election, peculiarly adapted to secure the overthrow of this accursed institution, and that under the administration of Mr. Lincoln we shall see the temple of liberty adorned, beautified, and made glorious by resting alone on the foundations of a constitution dedicating the country to freedom."[30]

James M. Scovel, who later attributed to Thaddeus Stevens the "purest man" quote, did not help matters when he delivered a partisan speech that charged lobbyists for the Camden and Amboy Railroad—an obsession of his—with influencing some members of the New Jersey senate to vote in favor of the amendment as part of a deal regarding the antimonopoly legislation in the U.S. Senate. Scovel's charge made voting in favor difficult for some Democrats who otherwise might have done so. By mid-March, New Jersey had rejected ratification.[31]

Lincoln's assassination quickened calls in the North that the amendment needed to be ratified swiftly. On April 19 Robert and Tad Lincoln, President Andrew Johnson, General Ulysses S. Grant, the cabinet, former vice president Hannibal Hamlin, and hundreds of mourners entered a candle-lit East Room to hold a funeral at the White House before bringing Lincoln's body to lie in state in the Capitol. Among the prayers offered came one from Methodist Episcopal bishop Matthew Simpson of Philadelphia, who appealed, "Around the remains of our loved President may we covenant together by every possible means to give ourselves to our country's service until every vestige of this rebellion shall have been wiped out, and until slavery, its cause, shall be forever eradicated." Unitarian reverend Cyrus A. Bartol of Boston blamed Lincoln's assassination on slavery, claiming, "That demon whispered in the actor's ear," but he assured "that slavery died more swiftly and surely by this very stroke" and exhorted his listeners, "Let our consolation be in . . . slavery's own unsparing destruction."[32]

A more simple statement came from Kentuckian Samuel Haycraft, who as a boy had known Lincoln's father. Haycraft wrote to William Herndon in June 1865 that he had opposed Lincoln's election but came around during his presidency to believe that "he was the very man for the place" and his assassination "one of the greatest calamities that could befall the nation & particularly the South." Haycraft claimed to have been "a Union man. a [*sic*] proslavery man—& wanted all things restored as they were at the Commencement of the war, but the South made the abolition of slavery a necessity & I am now willing for the Constitutional Amendment—It may be called fanaticism in me but it looks to me as if the Lord had raised up A Lincoln for the special purpose of blotting out Slavery."[33]

Lincoln's death had a direct impact on ratification in New York, where a Democratic minority in the assembly had earlier blocked it after the state senate had approved the measure. As Lincoln's funeral train neared Albany, these legislators realized it would be difficult to maintain opposition to an antislavery amendment. On April 22, four days before Lincoln's body arrived in Albany, enough Democrats voted in favor so that the Empire State gave its approval for ratification.[34]

Some mourners invoked Lincoln to argue for an expansive vision of what freedom would mean under the amendment. In Boston, Unitarian reverend James Freeman Clarke announced, "[The] revenge we shall take for the murder of Lincoln will be, to raise the loyal black population of the South not only to the position of freemen, but of voters; to shut out from power forever the leaders of the rebellion; to re-admit no Southern State into the Union until it has adopted a free-state constitution, and passed that anti-slavery amendment so dear to Abraham Lincoln's heart. We might not have insisted on these conditions,—perhaps it was necessary for Lincoln to die, to bring the nation to the point of demanding them." With somewhat more rage, Reverend R. H. Neale promised, "Mr. Lincoln was disposed to be lenient; but if, in their malignity, they dash the cup of kindness from his hand, they must not complain if the contents of the apocalyptic vial should not be poured out upon their land, till it shall consume every green thing, and turn a third part of the waters into blood. If they smite down their best friend, they must take the consequences." According to Neale, Lincoln "never would have consented to any civil disabilities because of color. The hand that signed the memorable proclamation never would have signed any document that did not contemplate the full citizenship of those who have proved themselves the worthiest portion of the Southern people."[35]

In Boston's Faneuil Hall on April 17, 1865, former state representative Peleg W. Chandler declared, "We must banish from the land

Thomas Nast's contrast between slavery on the left, including scenes showing the hunting of fugitives, selling slaves at auction, and branding and flogging, and freedom on the right, including a black mother sending her child to school and a black man receiving his pay. Thomas Nast, "Emancipation," 1865. Library of Congress.

every relic of barbarism. We must colonize the country with respectable men. We must organize school-districts and build schoolhouses, and send schoolmasters, and spelling books, and the New England Primer, and ministers of the Gospel, and Bibles." Charles G. Loring, who would later help found Boston's Museum of Fine Arts, found God's hand in making Washington "father of his country" and Lincoln "the father of his country in her new birth to a Union founded on still broader principles of law, freedom, and humanity."[36]

In London, prominent reformer Reverend Newman Hall, who would raise funds for London's Lincoln Memorial Tower as an international monument to the president, delivered a sermon a month after Lincoln's assassination that echoed what some of the Boston speakers had said: "At least this good has resulted from the crime,—that if there was previously any possibility of compromise, any disposition, for the sake of union and peace, to deal gently with the slavery question, and not immediately and completely to let the captive go free, there will be none now. . . . No! the death of Lincoln is the final knell of slavery."[37]

On June 1, 1865, Charles Sumner delivered a eulogy in Boston's Music Hall, crediting Washington with securing independence and Lincoln with championing the Declaration of Independence. Sumner, too, saw divine intervention in Lincoln's death in that it "set a sacred, irreversible seal upon the good he had done" and "put Emancipation beyond all mortal question." Moreover, for Sumner, Lincoln in death still spoke to America, "summoning his countrymen *back to the truths that are in the Declaration of Independence*."[38]

Sumner did not praise without some reproach, criticizing Lincoln's slowness in some respects. "Perhaps, his courage to apply truth was not always equal to his clearness in seeing it," Sumner announced, continuing, "Perhaps, the heights that he gained in conscience were not always sustained in conduct." While Sumner credited that Lincoln "was at all times willing to learn and not ashamed to change," adding that "before death he had already expressed his desire that the suffrage should be extended to colored persons in certain cases," he also criticized that Lincoln's position conflicted with "that very principle of Equality for which he so often contended."[39]

Sumner told audience members that slavery caused Lincoln's death, and he called on them to direct their vengeance against it by promoting black suffrage. "The demon of Caste takes the place of the demon of Slavery. In setting ourselves against this fearful demon, we only follow the solemn behests of the great Declaration, of which our martyred president was the champion." Sumner did not focus on the past work of the Thirteenth Amendment, already on its way toward ratification, but toward the future Fifteenth Amendment, exhorting his listeners, "Fellow-citizens, your task is before you."[40]

African Americans also invoked Lincoln's memory in helping to define what freedom meant. A convention of black Illinoisans who assembled in October 1866 included in an address to the American people that "a voice from the tomb of the martyred Lincoln seems now to reach the national ear, saying, 'The hour is come in which to enfranchise the colored American people, that they may "help you keep the jewel of liberty in the family of freedom."' . . . And in the memorable words of departed excellence and worth, it is within your competency to 'meanly lose, or nobly save, the last best hope of the earth!'"[41]

Few graphic images of the Thirteenth Amendment exist. After Lincoln's assassination, depictions of the Union's martyr in connection with the Emancipation Proclamation proliferated to the short shrift of the Thirteenth Amendment. Lincoln appeared, however, on several 1870 prints commemorating the ratification of the Fifteenth Amendment that provided black males with the ballot. These depictions frequently showed black people experiencing freedom: learning at school, working at trades, and voting. In what he would probably find a very meaningful validation of his efforts, Lincoln's words and actions shaped legal developments, and thus real lives, after his death, something that these images recognized.[42]

To this day, National Freedom Day commemorates Lincoln's support for the Thirteenth Amendment. Richard W. Wright, a young Georgia slave at the time of the amendment's ratification, later attended school in Atlanta and moved to Philadelphia. Wright organized Freedom Day in Philadelphia, selecting February 1, 1942, as its first observation, based on the date Lincoln signed the amendment

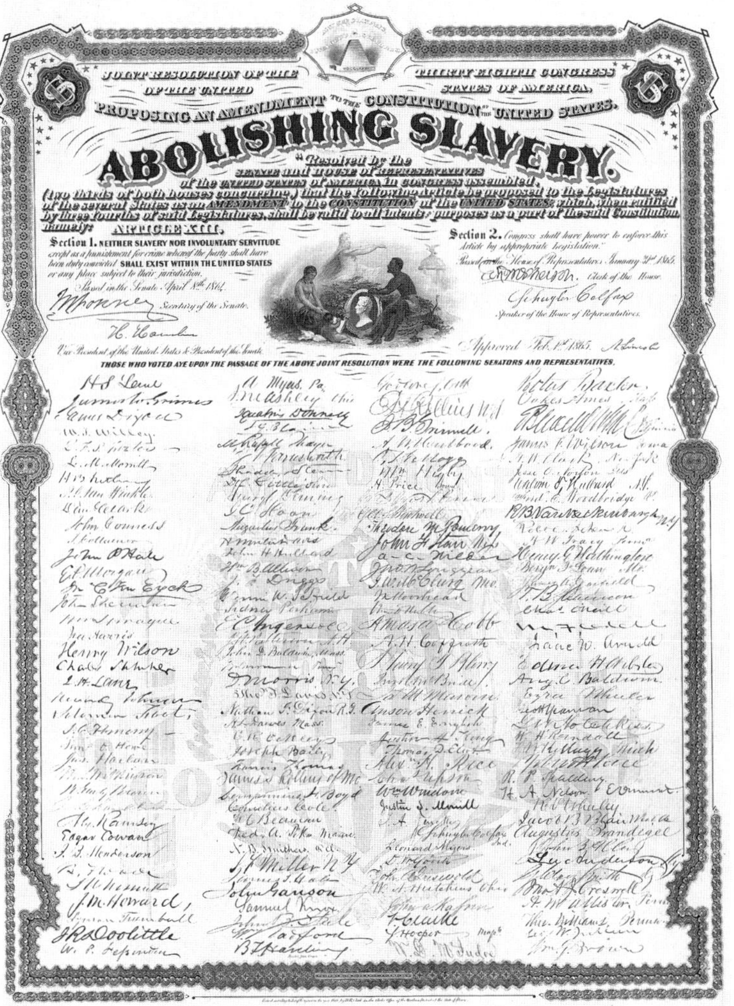

The text of the Thirteenth Amendment along with signatures of those who voted in its favor. At the top, a black man, his chains broken on the ground, holds a portrait of Lincoln while a black woman reads with a child. D. R. Clark, "Abolishing Slavery," 1868. Library of Congress.

A broadside celebrating the Fifteenth Amendment. In the middle, black men, including soldiers, parade in Baltimore to celebrate the amendment. Flanking this image are columns identified as Education and Science, each topped with a ballot box. To the left of the main panel are black children learning from a teacher of their race, and to the right are black craftsmen at work. At top, a portrait of Lincoln is flanked by those of President Ulysses S. Grant, Vice President Schuyler Colfax, John Brown, and Judge Hugh Lenox Bond. At bottom are portraits of black leaders Frederick Douglass and Mississippi senator Hiram R. Revels. G. F. Kahl, "The Fifteenth Amendment and Its Results," 1870. Library of Congress.

resolution. In later years the city's commemoration included speeches by Thurgood Marshall and Martin Luther King Jr., and an annual ceremony that continues to be held includes the laying of a wreath at the Liberty Bell. Wright successfully urged Congress to make February 1 National Freedom Day, though he died before President Harry S. Truman signed the act in 1948.[43]

CONCLUSION

Before the Civil War, Lincoln had identified some of the ways slavery harmed the United States and its people. Slavery was the one issue divisive enough that it could tear apart the Union. Eliminating for slaves their personal freedom, and all that flowed from it, slavery substituted for them instead all the dehumanizing elements that bondage entailed. Slavery also trampled on the rights of white Americans, causing its defenders to tamp down freedom of speech in the South for fear of any meaningful discussion of antislavery thought. On both counts, slavery mocked the ideals of the United States and made hypocritical its self-identity as a global beacon of republicanism. Moreover, Lincoln and Republicans argued that slavery stunted economic development in the South, in contrast to the productivity of the free states. Only slavery's death would strengthen the United States as a nation-state by removing the one issue that threatened to shatter it and by making it one that could live up to the ideals of the Declaration of Independence.[1]

At first Lincoln rejected the idea that the Constitution could be amended, and, working within the framework of that charter as contemporary Americans understood it, he argued for quarantining slavery. Wartime events eventually led Lincoln to support the idea of amendment, and after the 1864 election, he crafted his political victory into a mandate for constitutional change. In hindsight, Lincoln found the amendment the perfect solution in that it allowed him to resolve the tension between slavery and the ideals of the Declaration of Independence while remaining faithful to the Constitution and the will of the people. In contrast to Franklin Delano Roosevelt's threat to "pack the Court" to effect constitutional change or modern discussion about working outside of Article V to do so, Lincoln relied on the Constitution's amendment process. This method was national but involved the states, and it allowed the people to express their will but tempered it through the representative process. The Thirteenth Amendment also adjusted the doctrine and practice of federalism but shielded it at the same time from more threatening Radical Republican proposals, and it preserved the separation of powers created by the Constitution. By including Confederate states in the ratification process, Lincoln not only remained consistent with his position that they had never left the Union in the first place but also hoped their participation would facilitate the restoration of practical political relations within the country. Lincoln also likely felt that allowing white Southerners a voice in the national process of abolition might make the end of slavery easier for them to accept.[2]

Lincoln's election in 1860 forced the issue of making a national determination about slavery, and various decisions he made afterward—from holding firm to the 1860 Republican platform to signing the Emancipation Proclamation, and from his eloquent words in favor of freedom to his support and work for the Thirteenth Amendment—guided the outcome of the constitutional debate. Lincoln's presidential leadership helped shape the people's will while he maintained his fidelity, and that of the United States, to the form and substance of the Constitution.

Despite its simple wording, the Thirteenth Amendment profoundly changed the Constitution and thought about it. On one level, the amendment performed some obvious tasks: it abolished slavery and made the Constitution an explicitly antislavery document, rendered moot the Fugitive Slave and Three-Fifths Clauses, and eliminated the concept, outlined by Roger Taney in his *Dred Scott* ruling, that the Fifth Amendment protected property in human beings. Lincoln before the war had called for Taney's *Dred Scott* ruling to be overruled, and, along with the amendment that followed it, the Thirteenth Amendment did just that.

In the process, the Thirteenth Amendment helped unite the American people in a stronger nation-state. For Lincoln, the Union was "perpetual," yet slavery threatened his nationalistic vision. When Lincoln spoke of maintaining the Union, by necessity he would have required the destruction of the one institution that almost tore it apart. Moreover, with the Thirteenth Amendment, Lincoln envisioned a country unified in free labor economics and the ideals of the Declaration of Independence at the core of its nationalism. In 1854 Lincoln had announced to an audience in Peoria, Illinois, "Let us re-adopt the Declaration of Independence, and with it, the practices, and policy, which harmonize with it. Let north and south—let all Americans—let all lovers of liberty everywhere—join in the great and good work. If we do this, we shall not only have saved the Union; but we shall have so saved it, as to make, and to keep it, forever worthy of the saving." In Chicago in 1858 Lincoln exhorted Americans to "unite as one people throughout this land, until we shall once more stand up declaring that all men are created equal." Lincoln recognized that which his critic Wendell Phillips warned about in December 1861 in a speech urging Congress to pass legislation abolishing slavery: "Peace with an unchanged Constitution would leave us to stand like Mexico. States married, not matched; chained together, not melted into one; foreign nations aware of our hostility, and interfering to embroil, rob, and control us."[3]

The Thirteenth Amendment led to other shifts. A lot of antebellum constitutional discussion focused on the boundaries of the federal government, whether the topic involved banks or internal improvements. The twelve amendments enacted during the Founding era dealt with the mechanics of the federal government or limiting it. Where Thomas Jefferson and Andrew Jackson feared the threat the power of the federal government could pose to personal liberty, Lincoln, as a Whig, leaned toward a more robust, if still limited, use of federal power. The Thirteenth Amendment relied on that power in defense of freedom; it not only incorporated natural law freedom into the Constitution but also granted the federal government authority to use positive law to protect it.[4]

The first piece of legislation enacted pursuant to the Thirteenth Amendment, the Civil Rights Act of 1866, defined all persons born in the United States as citizens regardless of race or color except for Native Americans, because their allegiance lay with their tribal nation. The act, portions of which are still in effect today, held that national citizens, "of every race and color, without regard to any previous condition of slavery or involuntary servitude, except as a punishment for crime whereof the party shall have been duly convicted, shall have the same right, in every State and Territory in the United States, to make and enforce contracts, to sue, be parties, and give evidence, to inherit, purchase, lease, sell, hold, and convey real and personal property, and to full and equal benefit of all laws and proceedings for the security of person and property, as is enjoyed by white citizens, and shall be subject to like punishment, pains, and penalties, and to none other, any law, statute, ordinance, regulation, or custom, to the contrary notwithstanding." The act also authorized removing to the federal courts civil and criminal cases where persons could not enforce in their state or local court the rights it secured to them.[5]

The act strengthened the American nation-state by providing a definition of national citizenship rights in the law for the first time, and it did so in a color-blind fashion. Moreover, in harmony with the Republican Party's free labor ideology, the act included economic rights of contract and property and access to justice (one cannot enforce a contract, for example, without being able to bring a lawsuit) so as to provide white and black Americans with admission to the growing capitalist economy as a right of citizenship. The act thus recognized a greater role for the federal government in defining and protecting citizenship rights, in contrast to the almost wholly state-based model that came before it. At the same time, Republicans intended by the act that within each state every person would enjoy the same laws protecting personal and property rights. The Thirteenth Amendment altered the doctrine and practice of federalism but did not mean its abandonment.[6]

The process of constitutional reform in 1864–65 also helped change views that amending the Constitution defiled that document and its drafters. Enacting the Thirteenth Amendment permitted

Americans to see the Constitution as something that could be revised, and it opened up use of the amendment process for future generations. Lincoln accepted this position gradually, and one can see in him during the course of the war a transformation from opposing amendment to recognizing that cautious revision sometimes was necessary. Future generations would more easily turn to constitutional amendments, including to overturn Supreme Court decisions, specifically the Sixteenth Amendment (authorizing a national income tax), the Twenty-Fourth Amendment (prohibiting poll taxes), and the Twenty-Sixth Amendment (lowering the voting age to eighteen).[7]

The Thirteenth Amendment also resolved the conflicted meaning of liberty in the antebellum United States. In a speech in Baltimore in April 1864, Lincoln observed, "We all declare for liberty; but in using the same *word* we do not all mean the same *thing*." Lincoln explained: "With some the word liberty may mean for each man to do as he pleases with himself, and the product of his labor; while with others the same word may mean for some men to do as they please with other men, and the product of other men's labor." Lincoln illustrated his point with an analogy: "The shepherd drives the wolf from the sheep's throat, for which the sheep thanks the shepherd as a *liberator*," Lincoln elaborated, "while the wolf denounces him for the same act as the destroyer of liberty, especially as the sheep was a black one. Plainly the sheep and the wolf are not agreed upon a definition of the word liberty; and precisely the same difference prevails to-day among us human creatures." The Thirteenth Amendment, then, defined liberty to comport with free labor concepts; it rejected the definition provided by slaveholders concerned with their right in their human property in favor of a definition that included protection for property but also personal freedom and individual volition. For Lincoln and other Republicans, these protections applied to all Americans regardless of race or color. In response to Democratic proslavery and racist thought, Republican challengers now enshrined in the Constitution the language of freedom from which many of them looked, in varying degrees, toward a more egalitarian United States based on color-blind citizenship.[8]

At the same time, the language of the Thirteenth Amendment remained vague in its practical meaning, though it granted Congress the authority to enforce it with appropriate legislation, a provision that fit with Lincoln's views about the role of the legislature. Besides its political practicality, Lincoln probably liked the vagueness of the provision because it would allow Congress some room for interpretation. Similar to debates during the Founding about whether enumerating rights precluded those not mentioned in the Constitution, the vagueness of the Thirteenth Amendment not only helped get it passed through Congress and ratified by the states but also avoided the limitations of over-specificity.

Lincoln provided clues as to what he likely thought the amendment meant. For example, Lincoln defined several times his vision of a free labor society. In Milwaukee in 1859, Lincoln announced, "The prudent, penniless beginner in the world, labors for wages awhile, saves a surplus with which to buy tools or land, for himself; then labors on his own account another while, and at length hires another new beginner to help him." Lincoln quoted this sentence verbatim in his first Annual Message to Congress, adding after it, "This is the just, and generous, and prosperous system, which opens the way to all—gives hope to all, and consequent energy, and progress, and improvement of condition to all." In Milwaukee, Lincoln went on, "If any continue through life in the condition of the hired laborer, it is not the fault of the system, but because of either a dependent nature which prefers it, or improvidence, folly, or singular misfortune." Lincoln also emphasized the need for "universal education," that "every head should be cultivated, and improved, by whatever will add to its capacity for performing its charge." For Lincoln, "by the best cultivation of the physical world, beneath and around us; and the intellectual and moral world within us, we shall secure an individual, social, and political prosperity and happiness, whose course shall be onward and upward, and which, while the earth endures, shall not pass away."[9]

Lincoln cast the Civil War as defending this free labor vision for all people. On July 4, 1861, he asserted, "On the side of the Union, it is a struggle for maintaining in the world, that form, and substance of government, whose leading object is, to elevate the condition of men—to lift artificial weights from all shoulders—to clear the paths of laudable pursuit for all—to afford all, an unfettered start, and a fair chance, in the race of life." And in August 1864, in a speech to an Ohio infantry regiment that had completed its service, he identified why he thought it so important the Union win the war: "It is in order that each of you may have through this free government which we have enjoyed, an open field and a fair chance for your industry, enterprise and intelligence; that you may all have equal privileges in the race of life, with all its desirable human aspirations. It is for this the struggle should be maintained."[10]

Lincoln wanted an open field for economic advancement for anyone who worked for it, and he applied this concept through the Thirteenth Amendment to Americans of all races and colors. In supporting wartime legislation such as the Homestead Act and Morrill Act, Lincoln expressed his Whiggish perspective that the federal government could help people help themselves in pursuing economic success and freedom. The Thirteenth Amendment, then, combined impulses of the Jacksonian emphasis on the self-made individual with the Whiggish view that government should encourage people who wished to work toward this goal.

Historian George M. Fredrickson questions how Lincoln would have addressed the Black Codes passed across the South in the immediate aftermath of the Civil War. Black Codes gave African Americans some rights but heavily restricted them at the same time, including labor provisions that governed contracts and wages, licensing at exorbitant fees for certain crafts or occupations, and the arrest of black people who without "good cause" quit their employment. Noting Lincoln's strong commitment to federalism, Fredrickson claims that, while one would like to think Lincoln would have recognized the unfairness of the Black Codes, he would not have been able to address them without abandoning his constitutional thinking.[11]

More likely, Lincoln would have supported the Civil Rights Act of 1866, passed by Congress in direct response to the Black Codes, as legislation appropriate to enforcing the Thirteenth Amendment. Lincoln also likely would have noted that the act altered but maintained federalism. Allowing the legislature broad latitude within certain limits, moreover, comported with Lincoln's political philosophy.

Furthermore, Lincoln had signaled that, in his mind, the amendment meant more than just an end to chattel slavery when he called it "a King's cure for all the evils." Lincoln had in March 1865 signed an act creating the Freedmen's Bureau, a temporary agency that would involve itself in trying to enforce contracts and promote education for black people. In his last speech, Lincoln spoke of enfranchising black men. These acts and statements emphasize Lincoln's shift from concern that black and white people could not live side by side to a vision that involved integration and equality before the law. In a roundabout way, Lincoln had a hand in holding constitutional the Civil Rights Act of 1866: he appointed the Supreme Court justice Noah Swayne, who upheld the act in his capacity as a circuit court judge.[12]

The Supreme Court has helped shape the boundaries of the Thirteenth Amendment's applicability. In the *Civil Rights Cases* (1883), the Supreme Court held that the Thirteenth Amendment established "universal civil and political freedom throughout the United States," that its enforcement provision "clothes Congress with power to pass all laws necessary and proper for abolishing all badges and incidents of slavery in the United States," and that it applies to private individuals and state acts. The Fourteenth Amendment, by contrast, applies only to state action. On the other hand, the Court also determined that the Thirteenth Amendment applies only to civil and political, not to social, rights and declared that segregation from public accommodations was not a badge or vestige of slavery. Justice John Marshall Harlan, the lone dissenter in this case as he would be in *Plessy v. Ferguson*, argued for a broader reading of the Thirteenth Amendment.[13]

In the context of the post–World War II civil rights movement, the Supreme Court broadened the Thirteenth Amendment's applicability. In *Jones v. Alfred H. Mayer Company* (1968), the Court held that the amendment authorized Congress to eliminate private housing discrimination and "all racial barriers to the acquisition of real and personal property." The Court also set out a deferential standard of review in considering legislation passed under the Thirteenth Amendment: "Surely Congress has the power under the Thirteenth

Amendment rationally to determine what are the badges and the incidents of slavery, and the authority to translate that determination into effective legislation." Holding that "when racial discrimination herds men into ghettos and makes their ability to buy property turn on the color of their skin, then it too is a relic of slavery," the Court added, "The freedom that Congress is empowered to secure under the Thirteenth Amendment includes the freedom to buy whatever a white man can buy, the right to live wherever a white man can live. If Congress cannot say that being a free man means at least this much, then the Thirteenth Amendment made a promise the Nation cannot keep." *Jones* prohibited racial discrimination in the making and enforcement of contracts, including as to the sale or rental of property, followed by *Runyon v. McCrary* (1976), in which the Supreme Court applied this concept to private schools to hold that they could not discriminate on the basis of race.[14]

Today, legal commentators continue to debate the parameters of the second section of the Thirteenth Amendment. On one hand, this provision could be read to create a very broad congressional power to address human rights issues. On the other hand, the doctrines of federalism and the separation of powers still apply. Lawmakers knew about *McCulloch v. Maryland* (1819), and the role it preserved for judicial review, when they drafted the Thirteenth Amendment. The *Jones* court quoted from *McCulloch*. Not only does Congress's power to legislate under Section 2 of the amendment have limits, but the courts play an important role in helping to define the law under the Thirteenth Amendment.[15]

Recent law review articles argue for applying the Thirteenth Amendment across a range of issues, including race-based hate speech, racial profiling, race-based peremptory jury challenges, conditions in black communities, race disparities in capital punishment and health care, reproductive freedom, sexual discrimination and harassment, and discrimination of homosexuals. Since 2010 the White House has proclaimed January National Slavery and Human Trafficking Prevention Month but extends it to culminate on National Freedom Day on February 1, to bring attention to an issue to which the Thirteenth Amendment undoubtedly applies.[16]

Some law professors have called on Congress to use the Thirteenth Amendment to address labor issues beyond those with direct parallels with slavery, arguing that it contains broader language to deal with such concerns than does the Commerce Clause, on which Congress typically relies to do so. Before the New Deal, labor activists saw union rights to organize, boycott, and strike as coming from the First and Thirteenth Amendments, but legal professionals, wary of broad rights arguments, increasingly adopted the Commerce Clause as the preferred avenue to enact labor-related legislation. Law professor Alexander Tsesis further identifies the Thirteenth Amendment as the constitutional provision best suited to deal with civil rights and individual liberties. Tsesis notes that the Fourteenth Amendment addresses only state-sponsored matters, not private ones, and where an overriding public interest can permit the state to infringe on rights otherwise protected by the Fourteenth Amendment, even a compelling state interest does not justify a state or private infringement under the Thirteenth Amendment. Moreover, Tsesis observes, the Commerce Clause, though "grafted ingeniously into the civil rights arena," needs an economic component to make it apply, whereas the Thirteenth Amendment does not.[17]

On the other hand, some scholars warn against overextending the amendment's applicability, wherein people try to apply it to matters they find undesirable but that are unrelated to slavery or involuntary servitude. Even under the deferential standard of judicial review articulated by the Supreme Court in its *McCulloch* ruling, means must be "appropriate" within the Thirteenth Amendment to be held constitutional pursuant to it. Furthermore, in its ruling in *City of Boerne v. Flores* (1997), which addressed the Fourteenth Amendment's enforcement provision, the Supreme Court sent a message that it intends to continue patrolling the boundaries of congressional authority. While different lines of case law apply to interpreting the Thirteenth and Fourteenth Amendments, one can assume from its *City of Boerne* ruling that the Supreme Court would give broad deference to Congress in legislating pursuant to the Thirteenth Amendment but would strike down more radical theories about its applicability to issues unrelated to slavery or involuntary servitude.[18]

Thus, the Thirteenth Amendment works as Lincoln likely hoped it would. As the "King's cure for all the evils" wrought by slavery, Lincoln understood how the amendment could operate broadly to address various issues surrounding freedom and its definition. At the same time, the Thirteenth Amendment preserved the constitutional equilibrium: the president's powerful voice can encourage certain readings of it, Congress can articulate the will of the people through legislation enacted pursuant to its second section, and the Supreme Court can ensure that such legislation is appropriate to its enforcement. If the people disagree with the actions of any branch, they can turn to elections or the amendment process for corrective action. The Thirteenth Amendment accomplished Lincoln's goal of bringing the Founding charter closer to the ideals of the Declaration of Independence while preserving its fundamental structure. For someone like Lincoln, who so greatly valued both the Declaration of Independence and the Constitution, there could be no more fitting monument to his legacy.

ACKNOWLEDGMENTS

APPENDIX

NOTES

BIBLIOGRAPHY

INDEX

ACKNOWLEDGMENTS

My special thanks go to Patrick Cento and Emily Dixon for their excellent research assistance and intellectual curiosity. I also thank Ellen Keith of the Chicago History Museum Research Center, Kate Collins of the David M. Rubenstein Rare Book and Manuscript Library at Duke University, and Melinda Wallington and Lori Birrell of the Department of Rare Books and Special Collections at Rush Rhees Library at the University of Rochester for sending me copies of requested documents so quickly, and Cheryl Gunselman of the Manuscripts, Archives, and Special Collections of the Washington State University Libraries for graciously reviewing for me Joseph Baily's papers regarding a biographical question.

I thank William C. Harris for his very helpful comments on the manuscript. Richard W. Etulain and Sylvia Frank Rodrigue provided valuable suggestions as well as their enthusiasm for this project. Any errors are my responsibility alone.

Finally, my deepest gratitude goes to my family for their love and encouragement (especially to my father for closely reading several versions of my manuscript and offering me excellent comments) and to all of my friends for their support and fellowship.

APPENDIX

Article V of the Constitution

The Congress, whenever two thirds of both Houses shall deem it necessary, shall propose Amendments to this Constitution, or, on the Application of the Legislatures of two thirds of the several States, shall call a Convention for proposing Amendments, which, in either Case, shall be valid to all Intents and Purposes, as Part of this Constitution, when ratified by the Legislatures of three fourths of the several States, or by Conventions in three fourths thereof, as the one or the other Mode of Ratification may be proposed by the Congress; Provided that no Amendment which may be made prior to the Year One thousand eight hundred and eight shall in any Manner affect the first and fourth Clauses in the Ninth Section of the first Article; and that no State, without its Consent, shall be deprived of its equal Suffrage in the Senate.

Thirteenth Amendment

Section 1. Neither slavery nor involuntary servitude, except as a punishment for crime whereof the party shall have been duly convicted, shall exist within the United States, or any place subject to their jurisdiction.

Section 2. Congress shall have power to enforce this article by appropriate legislation.

NOTES

Introduction

1. Lincoln, "Speech at Peoria, Illinois," October 16, 1854, *Collected Works* (hereafter *CW*) 2:274; "Seventh and Last Debate with Stephen A. Douglas at Alton, Illinois," October 15, 1858, ibid., 3:313; "Speech at Hartford, Connecticut," March 5, 1860, ibid., 4:5–6; "Response to a Serenade," February 1, 1865, ibid., 8:255.
2. Lincoln, "Speech on the Sub-Treasury," December [26], 1839, ibid., 1:169.
3. Lincoln, "Speech at Peoria, Illinois," October 16, 1854, ibid., 2:255; "Fourth Debate with Stephen A. Douglas at Charleston, Illinois," September 18, 1858, ibid., 3:180–81; "Seventh and Last Debate with Stephen A. Douglas at Alton, Illinois," October 15, 1858, ibid., 3:313; "To Albert G. Hodges," April 4, 1864, ibid., 7:281.
4. Lincoln, "Speech at Peoria, Illinois," October 16, 1854, ibid., 2:255.

1. Before the Presidency

1. Lincoln, "Address before the Young Men's Lyceum of Springfield, Illinois," January 27, 1838, *CW*, 1:109.
2. Ibid., 1:109, 111.
3. Ibid., 1:112, 115.
4. Lincoln, "Message to Congress in Special Session," July 4, 1861, ibid., 4:427.
5. "Exposition and Protest," in *Statutes at Large of South Carolina*, 1:269–70.
6. Polk, Veto Message, August 3, 1846, in *Veto Messages*, 187; Veto Message, December 15, 1847, 207.
7. *Appendix to the Congressional Globe* (hereafter *CG*), 30th Cong., 1st Sess., 710 (June 20, 1848). The version of this speech reprinted in *CW*, 1:480–90, differs slightly.
8. Lincoln, "To the Editor of the *Sangamo Journal*," June 13, 1836, *CW*, 1:48; "Speech in U.S. House of Representatives on the Presidential Question," July 27, 1848, ibid., 1:506; "Speech at Boston, Massachusetts," September 15, 1848, ibid., 2:5; Holt, *American Whig Party*, 310.
9. *CG*, 25th Cong., 3rd Sess., 205 (February 25, 1839); Vorenberg, *Final Freedom*, 11, 12.
10. *CG*, 31st Cong., 1st Sess., 1349 (July 6, 1850); Kyvig, *Explicit and Authentic Acts*, 145.

11. Lincoln, "Speech at Kalamazoo, Michigan," August 27, 1856, *CW*, 2:365, 366; "Address at Cooper Institute, New York City," February 27, 1860, ibid., 3:534–35; Vorenberg, *Final Freedom*, 15.
12. Lincoln, "Speech at Chicago, Illinois," July 10, 1858, *CW*, 2:494; "Protest in Illinois Legislature on Slavery," March 3, 1837, ibid., 1:75.
13. United States Congress, *Debates and Proceedings*, House of Representatives, 1st Cong., 2nd Sess., 1524 (March 23, 1790); Finkelman, "Lincoln," 353; Samito, *Becoming American under Fire*, 1.
14. Lincoln, "Speech at Elwood, Kansas," December 1, 1859, *CW*, 3:496.
15. Lincoln, "Speech at Peoria, Illinois," October 16, 1854, ibid., 2:255, 266, 268.
16. Lincoln, "Speech at Kalamazoo, Michigan," August 27, 1856, ibid., 2:361–66; "Seventh and Last Debate with Stephen A. Douglas at Alton, Illinois," October 15, 1858, ibid., 3:313; "Address at Cooper Institute, New York City," February 27, 1860, ibid., 4:522–550.
17. *Scott v. Sandford*, 60 U.S. 393, 426 (1857).
18. Lincoln, "Speech at Springfield, Illinois," June 26, 1857, *CW*, 2:401.
19. Lincoln, "Speech at Springfield, Illinois," July 17, 1858, ibid., 2:519.
20. Lincoln, "Speech at Cincinnati, Ohio," September 17, 1859, ibid., 2:460–61.
21. Lincoln, "Speech at a Republican Banquet, Chicago, Illinois," December 10, 1856, ibid., 2:385; "Washington's Farewell Address," September 17, 1796, in Richardson, *Compilation*, 1:209.

2. Secession Winter

1. *Proceedings of the First Three Republican National Conventions*, 131–32; Ames, *Proposed Amendments*, 354; Kyvig, *Explicit and Authentic Acts*, 146.
2. *Appendix to the CG*, 36th Cong., 2nd Sess., 4 (December 3, 1860).
3. Lincoln to Gilmer, December 15, 1860, *CW*, 4:151–52; Holzer, *Lincoln President-Elect*, 157.
4. Lincoln to Trumbull, December 10, 1860, *CW*, 4:149–50; to Kellogg, December 11, 1860, ibid., 4:150; to Washburne, December 13, 1860, ibid., 4:151; to Trumbull, December 17, 1860, ibid., 4:153; to William H. Seward, February 1, 1861, ibid., 4:183; Holzer, *Lincoln President-Elect*, 158.
5. Lincoln to Seward, December 8, 1860, *CW*, 4:148; Weed to Lincoln, December 11, 1860, Abraham Lincoln Papers at the Library of Congress (hereafter ALP); Lincoln to Weed, December 17, 1860, *CW*, 4:154; Seward to Lincoln, December 16, 1860, ALP.
6. *Report of the Committee of Thirteen*, 36th Cong., 2nd Sess., Rep. Com. No. 288, 1–5; *CG*, 36th Cong., 2nd Sess., 114 (December 18, 1860).

7. Lincoln, "Resolutions Drawn up for Republican Members of Senate Committee of Thirteen," [December 20, 1860], *CW*, 4:156–57; Lincoln to Trumbull, December 21, 1860, ibid., 4:158.
8. Seward to Lincoln, December 26, 1860, ALP.
9. *Report of the Committee of Thirteen*, 10–11; Seward to Lincoln, December 26, 1860, ALP.
10. Harris to Georgia General Assembly, December 17, 1860, quoted in Dew, *Apostles of Disunion*, 85; Benning, 25. See also letter of Stephen F. Hale, commissioner from Alabama, to Governor Beriah Magoffin of Kentucky, December 27, 1860, in Dew, *Apostles of Disunion*, 90–103.
11. Seward to Lincoln, December 26, and December 28, 1860, ALP; *Report of the Committee of Thirteen*, 14–19.
12. Lincoln to Trumbull, December 28, 1860, *CW*, 4:162; Lincoln to Green, December 28, 1860, ibid., 4:162–63; Holzer, *Lincoln President-Elect*, 174–76.
13. *New York Herald*, January 8, 1861, quoted in *CW*, 4:163; Green to Lincoln, January 7, 1861, ALP; Holzer, *Lincoln President-Elect*, 176. Green referred in his letter dated January 7, 1861, to a letter of Lincoln's dated December 31; no such letter has been found. Green likely meant Lincoln's letter dated December 28, 1860.
14. *CG*, 36th Cong., 2nd Sess., 341–44 (January 12, 1861); quotes are on 344.
15. Lincoln to Seward, January 19, 1861, *CW*, 4:176.
16. Lincoln to Green, December 28, 1860, ibid., 4:162; Lincoln, "Speech at Peoria, Illinois," October 16, 1854, ibid., 2:274.
17. Lincoln, "Speech at Pittsburgh, Pennsylvania," February 15, 1861, ibid., 4:213, 214.
18. *CG*, 36th Cong., 2nd Sess., 1364 (March 2, 1861); Vorenberg, *Final Freedom*, 20–21. For an argument that Lincoln drafted or otherwise supported the Corwin Amendment, see Lee, "Corwin Amendment."
19. Lincoln, "First Inaugural Address—Final Text," March 4, 1861, *CW*, 4:263, 264; Finkelman, "Lincoln," 353.
20. Lincoln, "First Inaugural Address—Final Text," March 4, 1861, *CW*, 4:265, 267.
21. Ibid., 4:268.
22. Ibid., 4:269–70.
23. Ibid., 4:270. See this discussion in a state context in *Opinion of the Justices*, 264 A.2d 342, 345 (Del. 1970).
24. Lincoln, "First Inaugural Address—First Edition and Revisions," *CW*, 4:260, 261.

25. Lincoln, "First Inaugural Address—Final Text," March 4, 1861, ibid., 4:270.
26. The form letter addressed to the governor of Florida was found recently at the Lehigh County Historical Society in Allentown, Pennsylvania. Lupton, "Abraham Lincoln and the Corwin Amendment."

3. Toward the Emancipation Proclamation

1. *Scott v. Sandford*, 60 U.S. at 450; Finkelman, "Lincoln," 379.
2. Lincoln, "Drafts of a Bill for Compensated Emancipation in Delaware," November 1861, *CW*, 5:29–30; Lincoln to James A. McDougal[l], March 14, 1862, ibid., 5:160–61.
3. Lincoln, "Message to Congress," March 6, 1862, ibid., 5:145–46.
4. Burlingame, *With Lincoln in the White House*, 73–74 (journal entry, March 9, 1862); Masur, *Lincoln's Hundred Days*, 41, 43.
5. Lincoln to McDougal[l], March 14, 1862, *CW*, 5:160–61; *CG*, 37th Cong., 2nd Sess., 1373–74 (March 26, 1862); Masur, *Lincoln's Hundred Days*, 45; 12 Stat. 617 (37th Cong., 2nd Sess., Joint Resolution No. 26).
6. 12 Stat. 376 (Washington, D.C.); 12 Stat. 432 (territories); *Scott v. Sandford*, 60 U.S. at 450.
7. Lincoln, "Appeal to Border State Representatives to Favor Compensated Emancipation," July 12, 1862, *CW*, 5:317–19.
8. Welles, *Diary of Gideon Welles*, 1:70–71; Welles, "History of Emancipation," 843.
9. Border State congressmen to Lincoln, July 14 and July 15, 1862, ALP; *CG*, 38th Cong., 2nd Sess., 531 (January 31, 1865).
10. Lincoln, "To the Senate and House of Representatives," July 14, 1862, *CW*, 5:324–25; Vorenberg, *Final Freedom*, 27.
11. Finkelman, "Lincoln," 361, 362, 371–72.
12. Lincoln, "Preliminary Emancipation Proclamation," September 22, 1862, *CW*, 5:433–36.
13. Lincoln, "To the Senate and House of Representatives," December 1, 1862, ibid., 5:529–30.
14. Ibid., 5:530–31.
15. Ibid., 5:531.
16. Ibid.
17. Ibid., 5:531–32.
18. Ibid., 5:532–34.
19. Ibid., 5:534–36.
20. Ibid., 5:536.
21. Ibid., 5:536–37.
22. Ibid., 5:537.
23. Chase to Lincoln, November 28, 1862, ALP.

24. All quotes in Masur, *Lincoln's Hundred Days*, 180–81.
25. *CG*, 37th Cong., 3rd Sess., 6 (December 4, 1862); 79 (December 11, 1862); 112 (December 17, 1862); 136 (December 18, 1862); 138–39 (December 19, 1862); 1293–94 (February 25, 1863) (Maryland).
26. Blaine, *Twenty Years*, 1:445–47; Cole, *Reminiscences*, 223.
27. *CG*, 37th Cong., 3rd Sess., 79 (December 11, 1862).
28. Neely, *Lincoln and the Triumph of the Nation*, 130–31; Masur, *Lincoln's Hundred Days*, 177.
29. *Liberator*, January 2, 1863.
30. Curtis, *Executive Power*; Levinson, "Was the Emancipation Proclamation Constitutional?"; Hofstadter, *American Political Tradition*, 132.
31. Finkelman, "Lincoln," 352, 386; Paulsen, "Emancipation Proclamation," 810–12.
32. Lincoln, "Preliminary Emancipation Proclamation," September 22, 1862, *CW*, 5:434; "Emancipation Proclamation," January 1, 1863, ibid., 6:28–30.

4. The Road to an Abolition Amendment

1. Lincoln to Conkling, August 26, 1863, *CW*, 6:407–9.
2. Lincoln, "Address Delivered at the Dedication of the Cemetery at Gettysburg," November 19, 1863, ibid., 7:23.
3. Sumner, *Our Domestic Relations*, 523–26; Vorenberg, *Final Freedom*, 41.
4. Sumner, *Our Domestic Relations*, 526.
5. Blair, *Speech*, 4, 5, 6, 17.
6. Lincoln to Banks, August 5, 1863, *CW*, 6:364–65; to Johnson, September 11, 1863, ibid., 6:440; Blair, *Speech*, 17.
7. Lincoln to Chase, September 2, 1863, *CW*, 6:428–29.
8. John Hay memorandum, September 30, 1863, in Burlingame, *At Lincoln's Side*, 64.
9. Swett to William H. Herndon, January 17, 1866, in Wilson and Davis, *Herndon's Informants*, 164.
10. Arnold to Lincoln, December 4, 1863, ALP.
11. All quotes in Vorenberg, *Final Freedom*, 44–46.
12. *New York Times*, September 16, 1861; Meagher, *Letters*, 2, 3, 5, 14.
13. Lincoln, "Annual Message to Congress," December 8, 1863, *CW*, 7:49, 51.
14. Chase to Lincoln, November 25, 1863, ALP; *In re Turner*, 24 F. Cas. 337 (Circuit Court, D. Maryland 1867).
15. Lincoln, "Annual Message to Congress," December 8, 1863, *CW*, 7:52–53.
16. Lincoln, "Proclamation of Amnesty and Reconstruction," December 8, 1863, ibid., 7:54–55.
17. Ibid., 7:55–56.

18. *CG*, 38th Cong., 1st Sess., 19, 21 (December 14, 1863); 145 (January 11, 1864); 521 (February 8, 1864).
19. Arnold, *Abraham Lincoln*, 468–69.
20. Defrees to Lincoln, February 7, 1864, *CW*, 7:172–73.
21. Lincoln to Defrees, February 8, 1864, ibid., 7:172; *CG*, 38th Cong., 1st Sess., 521 (February 8, 1865).
22. *Proceedings . . . Religious Amendment*, v–vii.
23. Lincoln to Steele, January 20, 1864, *CW*, 7:141–42; to Steele, January 27, 1864, ibid., 7:154–55; to Creswell, March 7, 1864, ibid., 7:226–27; to Creswell, March 17, 1864, ibid., 7:251; Wagandt, *Mighty Revolution*, 195.
24. Lincoln to Banks, August 5, 1863, *CW*, 6:364–65; "Annual Message to Congress," December 8, 1863, ibid., 7:52–53; "Proclamation of Amnesty and Reconstruction," December 8, 1863, ibid., 7:55–56.
25. Harris, *With Charity for All*, 183; Lincoln to Hahn, March 13, 1864, *CW*, 7:243; see also Lincoln to James S. Wadsworth, January 1864 [?], *CW*, 7:101–02.
26. *New York Times*, February 11, 1864; February 13, 1864.
27. Vorenberg, *Final Freedom*, 71, 91.
28. *CG*, 38th Cong., 1st Sess., 1196–1204 (March 19, 1864); Vorenberg, *Final Freedom*, 91.
29. *CG*, 38th Cong., 1st Sess., 1419–24 (April 5, 1864); *New York Times*, April 6, 1864; *CG*, 38th Cong., 1st Sess., 1459–65 (quote on 1463) (April 7, 1864); Wagandt, *Mighty Revolution*, 217.
30. Vorenberg, *Final Freedom*, 107, 109, 111, 112, 113.
31. McPherson, *Political History*, 413; Vorenberg, *Final Freedom*, 76.

5. Reelection and the Politics of Constitutional Change

1. Nicolay and Hay, *Abraham Lincoln*, 10:79; Brooks, *Washington in Lincoln's Time*, 152.
2. Lincoln, "Reply to Committee Notifying Lincoln of His Renomination," June 9, 1864, *CW*, 7:380–82; *New York Independent*, June 16, 1864, quoted in Nicolay and Hay, *Abraham Lincoln*, 10:79.
3. Goodrich to Lincoln, June 11, 1864, ALP.
4. Garrison to Francis W. Newman, July 15, 1864, in Garrison, *Letters*, 5:221, 223.
5. Ibid., 5:226.
6. *New York Times*, June 17, 1864; Vorenberg, *Final Freedom*, 136–39.
7. *CG*, 38th Cong., 1st Sess., 3357 (June 28, 1864).
8. 38th Cong., 1s Sess., H.R. 244.
9. Burlingame and Ettlinger, *Inside Lincoln's White House*, 217–18 (July 4, 1864, entry).

10. Ibid.; Bogue, *Earnest Men*, 245.
11. Lincoln, "Proclamation Concerning Reconstruction," July 8, 1864, *CW*, 7:433–34.
12. *New York Times*, August 9, 1864.
13. *CG*, 38th Cong., 2nd Sess., 180 (January 9, 1865); Nicolay to Theodore Tilton, September 6, 1864, ALP; Vorenberg, *Final Freedom*, 141–75.
14. Lincoln, "To Whom It May Concern," July 18, 1864, *CW*, 7:451; Strong diary entry, August 19, 1864, in Burlingame and Ettlinger, *Inside Lincoln's White House*, 364 n. 277.
15. Seward, *Remarks*, 6; Cox and Cox, *Politics, Principle, and Prejudice*, 3–4; Vorenberg, *Final Freedom*, 155–56. See, for instance, Lincoln, "Response to a Serenade," October 19, 1864, *CW*, 8:52–53, which addressed Seward's speech.
16. "Constitutional Amendment," 315, 321; Walker, *Letter of Hon. R. J. Walker*, 5, 14.
17. *Daily Advertiser*, October 7, 1864, in Patrick R. Guiney scrapbook, 12–13, in the Patrick R. Guiney Papers.
18. *Proceedings of the National Convention of Colored Men*, 48–49, 51.
19. Ibid., 51–61.
20. McPherson, *Political History*, 419–20; *Address of Democratic Members of Congress*, 7; Winthrop, *Great Speech*, 7, 9.
21. James O. Broadhead to Edward Bates, July 24, 1864; Benjamin F. Loan to Lincoln, September 8, 1864; Carl Schurz to Lincoln, October 1, 1864; Nicolay to Lincoln, October 10, 1864 and October 18, 1864; William L. Avery to Nicolay, November 2, 1864, all in ALP; Bates, *Diary*, 394; *New York Times*, June 17, 1864.
22. Wagandt, *Mighty Revolution*, 262–63; Lincoln to Hoffman, October 10, 1864, *CW*, 8:41; to Hoffman, October 15, 1864, ibid., 8:48–49.
23. Noah Brooks, dispatch of October 19, 1864, in the *Sacramento Union*, November 25, 1864, in Burlingame, *Lincoln Observed*, 138; Lincoln, "Reply to Maryland Union Committee," November 17, 1864, *CW*, 8:113.
24. Lincoln, "Response to a Serenade," October 19, 1864, *CW*, 8:52–53.
25. Wagandt, *Mighty Revolution*, 262–63; Lincoln, "Speech to Forty-second Massachusetts Regiment," October 31, 1864, *CW*, 8:84.
26. Noah Brooks, dispatch of November 2, 1864, in the *Sacramento Union*, December 2, 1864, in Burlingame, *Lincoln Observed*, 141–42.
27. Douglass, "The Final Test of Self-Government," in *Frederick Douglass Papers*, 4:33, 34, 36, 37.
28. Garrison to Oliver Johnson, November 26, 1864, in Garrison, *Letters*, 5:240; Jay, *Mr. Jay's Remarks*, 2, 3–4.

6. Getting the Amendment Resolution Passed

1. *CG*, 38th Cong., 2nd Sess. 138, 142 (January 6, 1865); Lincoln to Albert G. Hodges, April 4, 1864, *CW*, 7:281.
2. Lincoln, "Annual Message to Congress," December 6, 1864, *CW*, 8:149.
3. Ibid.
4. Vorenberg, *Final Freedom*, 179–80, 189–92.
5. *CG*, 38th Cong., 1st Sess., 2940–41 (June 14, 1864); Vorenberg, *Final Freedom*, 179–80, 189–92; Lincoln, "Speech at Pittsburgh, Pennsylvania," February 15, 1861, *CW*, 4:214.
6. Corbin to Lincoln, December 8, 1864; Henderson to Lincoln, October 12, 1864; King to Bates, November 15, 1864, all in ALP.
7. Corbin to Lincoln, December 8, 1864; Brown to Lincoln, March 2, 1865, both in ALP; *CG*, 38th Cong., 2nd Sess., 258–63 (January 13, 1865), 531 (January 31, 1865).
8. Oldroyd, *Lincoln Memorial*, 491–95; *CG*, 38th Cong., 2nd Sess., 258–261 (January 13, 1865).
9. Cox, *Union*, 310, 330; Baker, *Lives of the Governors of Minnesota*, 67; Cox, *Eight Years*, 397; Cox to Marble, December 7, 1864, quoted in Vorenberg, *Final Freedom*, 182.
10. Arnold, *Abraham Lincoln*, 469.
11. *CG*, 38th Cong., 1st Sess., App. 124–126 (June 14, 1864); John A. Griswold in the Biographical Directory of the United States Congress, http://bioguide.congress.gov/scripts/biodisplay.pl?index=G000486, accessed January 20, 2014; Sylvester, *History of Rensselaer Co.*, 272; *Harper's Weekly*, June 14, 1862; Weygant, *History*, 127. A George Odell wounded at Chancellorsville survived (Weygant, *History*, 129, 267).
12. Blair to Johnson, June 16, 1865, in Johnson, *Papers*, 8:247; William N. Bilbo to Lincoln, January 26, 1865, ALP.
13. Latham to Seward, February 23, 1861; January 25, 1864, William Henry Seward Papers; Cox and Cox, *Politics, Principle, and Prejudice*, 6–7, 11–12, 13–14.
14. Bilbo to Lincoln, November 22, 1864; January 26, 1865, ALP; Bilbo to Seward, February 1, 1865, Seward Papers.
15. Bilbo to Seward, November 1864; December 12, 1864; February 1, 1865, Seward Papers; Bilbo to Lincoln, January 26, 1865, ALP.
16. Bilbo to Seward, December 20, 1864; December 23, 1864; Jones to Seward, December 20, 1864, all in Seward Papers.
17. Latham to Seward, January 7, 1865; January 9, 1865, ibid.
18. Bilbo to Seward, January 10, 1865, ibid.; *New York Times*, January 12, 1865; Bilbo to Johnson, January 10, 1865, in Johnson, *Papers*, 7:381; Bilbo to Seward, January 14, 1865, Seward Papers.

19. Forney to Hart, January 11, 1865 (two letters); Latham to Seward, January 12, 1865; Bilbo to Seward, November 2, 1865, all in Seward Papers; Cox and Cox, *Politics, Principle, and Prejudice*, 15–16.
20. *CG*, 38th Cong., 2nd Sess., 189–202 (January 10, 1865); 221–25 (January 11, 1865) (quotes on 223).
21. Ibid., 139 (January 6, 1865); 192 (January 10, 1865); 239–41 (January 12, 1865).
22. Lincoln to Cox, January 31, 1865, *CW*, 8:249.
23. Bilbo to Johnson, January 14, 1865, in Johnson, *Papers*, 7:404.
24. Lincoln to Dix, January 20, 1865, *CW*, 8:226; Bilbo to Seward, January 23, 1863, Seward Papers.
25. Cox to Marble, December 7, 1864, quoted in Vorenberg, *Final Freedom*, 182; *New York World*, January 9, 1865, quoted in Cox and Cox, *Politics, Principle, and Prejudice*, 5–6.
26. Schell to Seward, January 23, 1865, Seward Papers, quoted in Cox and Cox, *Politics, Principle, and Prejudice*, 19.
27. Bilbo to Seward, January 26, 1865, Seward Papers; Richmond to Marble, January 23, 1865, quoted in Vorenberg, *Final Freedom*, 203.
28. Bilbo to Lincoln, January 26, 1865, ALP.
29. Vorenberg, *Final Freedom*, 183–85; Cox and Cox, *Politics, Principle, and Prejudice*, 20 n. 127, 240.
30. Bilbo to Seward, February 1, 1865, Seward Papers; Cox and Cox, *Politics, Principle, and Prejudice*, 20, 25.
31. Blair to Johnson, June 16, 1865, in Johnson, *Papers*, 8:247.
32. *New York Times*, January 8, 1865; *CG*, 38th Cong., 2nd Sess., 200 (January 10, 1865); Cox and Cox, *Politics, Principle, and Prejudice*, 30.
33. Blaine, *Twenty Years*, 1:534; Vorenberg, "Thirteenth Amendment Enacted," 180–81; Williams, *Judging Lincoln*, 134.

7. The Final Vote

1. *CG*, 38th Cong., 2nd Sess., 522–24 (January 31, 1865).
2. Ibid., 524–30.
3. Cox, *Eight Years*, 397–98.
4. Ashley to William H. Herndon, November 23, 1866, in Wilson and Davis, *Herndon's Informants*, 413–14; Schurz to his wife, February 1, 1865, in Schurz, *Intimate Letters*, 314–15.
5. Cox, *Eight Years*, 398.
6. Lincoln, "Pass for Francis P. Blair, Sr.," December 28, 1864, *CW*, 8:188; Blair to Davis, December 30, 1864 (two letters), ibid., 8:188–89; address made by Blair to Davis on January 12, 1865, ALP; Blair's memorandum of his meeting, ALP; Lincoln to Francis P. Blair, Sr., January 18, 1865, *CW*, 8:220–21; to the House of Representatives, February 10, 1865, *CW*, 8:275–76.

7. Lincoln to Alexander H. Stephens, John A. Campbell, and Robert M. T. Hunter, [January 30, 1865,] *CW*, 8:248; to the House of Representatives, February 10, 1865, ibid., 8:275–77.
8. Lincoln to Seward, January 31, 1865, ibid., 8:250–51; to the House of Representatives, February 10, 1865, ibid., 8:278.
9. Ashley to William H. Herndon, November 23, 1866, in Wilson and Davis, *Herndon's Informants*, 413–14; Peabody to Horace Mann Jr., [February 1865,] in the Horace Mann Hawthorne-Mann Family Correspondence.
10. Vorenberg, *Final Freedom*, 205.
11. Ibid., 207–8; Nicolay to Lincoln, January 31, 1865, ALP.
12. *CG*, 38th Cong., 2nd Sess., 530, 531 (January 31, 1865).
13. Ibid., 179 (January 9, 1865); Boutwell, *Reminiscences*, 2:36; Julian, *Political Recollections*, 250.
14. Bilbo to Johnson, January 10, 1865, in Johnson, *Papers*, 7:381; Schell to Frederick W. Seward, February 13, 1865, in Seward MS, quoted in Cox and Cox, *Politics, Principle, and Prejudice*, 24; Cox and Cox, *Politics, Principle, and Prejudice*, 28; Vorenberg, *Final Freedom*, 202–4.
15. Cox, *Union*, 329; Cox, *Eight Years*, 396–98.
16. Rice, *Reminiscences*, 585–86 (Alley), 338 (Colfax). Doris Kearns Goodwin credits this story in *Team of Rivals*, 687.
17. Dana, *Recollections*, 174–76.
18. Ibid., 176–77.
19. *CG*, 38th Cong., 1st Sess., 788 (February 24, 1864); 1166 (March 17, 1864). Earl S. Pomeroy discounts Dana's story in "Lincoln, the Thirteenth Amendment, and the Admission of Nevada," 365–67.
20. Vorenberg, *Final Freedom*, 199; Vorenberg, "Thirteenth Amendment Enacted," 184.
21. Blair to Johnson, June 16, 1865, in Johnson, *Papers*, 8:247; Herrick to Seward, New York, July 3, 1865, Seward MS; United States Congress, *Senate Executive Journal*, 38th Cong., 2nd sess., March 10, 1865, 14:274.
22. Herrick to Seward, New York, July 3, 1865, Seward MS.
23. Herrick to Seward, August 8, 1865; Nelson to Seward, July 29, 1865; Herrick to Seward, February 5, 1867, all in Seward MS.
24. United States Congress, *Senate Executive Journal*, 39th Cong., 1st sess., December 19, 1865, 14:304 (Yeaman nomination); ibid., January 25, 1866, 485 (Yeaman confirmation); ibid., January 29, 1866, 497 (Odell nomination); ibid., April 26, 1866, 752 (Odell confirmation); *Official Register*, 106; Joseph A. Wright to Andrew Johnson, September 7, 1865, in Johnson, *Papers*, 9:42 (referring to "your appointment of Odell"); Keller, "'That Which Congress So Nobly Began,'" 200; Williams, *Judging Lincoln*, 138; Cox and Cox, *Politics, Principle, and Prejudice*, 29.

Doris Kearns Goodwin says Odell agreed to change his vote and then received the navy agent post; he voted in favor in June 1864. Goodwin, *Team of Rivals*, 687.

25. *CG*, 38th Cong., 2nd sess., 270 (January 16, 1865); 790 (February 14, 1865); 814 (February 16, 1865); Gillette, *Jersey Blue*, 259–64; Vorenberg, *Final Freedom*, 200.
26. Nicolay memoranda dated January 18, 1865, quoted in Nicolay and Hay, *Abraham Lincoln*, 10:84–85.
27. Ibid., 10:85.
28. Boutwell, *Reminiscences*, 2:36; Riddle, *Recollections*, 325.
29. *CG*, 38th Cong., 2nd Sess., 152 (January 7, 1865); 530 (January 31, 1865); Bogue, *Earnest Men*, 253; Gillette, *Jersey Blue*, 301. Vorenberg finds it almost certain the railroad influenced Rogers's absence. Vorenberg, *Final Freedom*, 200–201.
30. *CG*, 38th Cong., 2nd Sess., 1008 (February 23, 1865); Bogue, *Earnest Men*, 253; Gillette, *Jersey Blue*, 301; Vorenberg, *Final Freedom*, 200–201.
31. Scovel, "Thaddeus Stevens," 550; Stevens, *Selected Papers*, 2:304 n. 1.
32. Riddle, *Recollections*, 325; *CG*, 38th Cong., 2nd Sess., 524 (January 31, 1865); Vorenberg, *Final Freedom*, 201–2.

8. Peace, Ratification, and the Thirteenth Amendment

1. Lincoln to Grant, February 1, 1865; Lincoln to Eckert, February 1, 1865, both in ALP.
2. Lincoln, "Resolution Submitting the Thirteenth Amendment to the States," February 1, 1865, *CW*, 8:253; Rhodehamel and Kaller, "Census of Copies," 97–98; Seward to Lincoln, February 5, [1865,] ALP.
3. Andrew to Lincoln, February 1, 1865, ALP.
4. *CG*, 38th Cong., 2nd Sess. 588 (February 4, 1865); 631 (February 7, 1865). The case was *Hollingsworth v. Virginia*, 3 U.S. (3 Dall.) 378 (1798).
5. Goodrich to Lincoln, March 1, 1865, ALP.
6. Oglesby to Lincoln, February 1, 1865; Lamon and Baker to Lincoln, February 1, 1865, both in ALP.
7. Lincoln, "Response to a Serenade," February 1, 1865, *CW*, 8:254–55.
8. Lincoln, "To the House of Representatives," February 10, 1865, ibid., 8:281–83.
9. Ibid., 8:283–85.
10. Stephens, *Constitutional View*, 2:611–12; Campbell, *Reminiscences*, 6–7, 13.
11. Lincoln, "To the House of Representatives," February 10, 1865, *CW*, 8:284–85.
12. Stephens, *Constitutional View*, 2:614–15; Campbell, *Reminiscences*, 13.
13. Stephens, *Constitutional View*, 2:617; Campbell, *Reminiscences*, 16.

14. Campbell, *Reminiscences*, 17–18; *New York Tribune*, February 9, 1865, quoted in Vorenberg, "Thirteenth Amendment Enacted," 189; Rable, *Confederate Republic*, 292–94.
15. Nicolay and Hay, *Abraham Lincoln*, 10:79.
16. Lincoln to Bramlette, February 5, 1865, *CW*, 8:260; Seward to Lincoln, February 5, 1865, ALP.
17. Lincoln, "To the Senate and House of Representatives," February 5, 1865, *CW*, 8:260–61.
18. Ibid., 8:261; Usher, "Abraham Lincoln"; Welles, *Diary*, February 6, 1865, quoted in Nicolay and Hay, *Abraham Lincoln*, 10:136.
19. Peabody to Horace Mann Jr., [February 1865,] Horace Mann Hawthorne-Mann Family Correspondence.
20. *CG*, 38th Cong., 2nd Sess., 588 (February 4, 1865); 1010 (February 23, 1865).
21. Lincoln, "Last Public Address," April 11, 1865, *CW*, 8:400–403.
22. Ibid., 8:403; Donald, *Lincoln*, 588.
23. Lincoln, "Last Public Address," April 11, 1865, *CW*, 8:403–4.
24. *CG*, 40th Cong., 2nd Sess., 878 (January 31, 1868); Bates, *Diary*, 526 (December 21, 1865); McPherson, *Hand-book of Politics for 1872*, 204, 210.
25. Bramlette to Lincoln, March 2, 1865, ALP; Vorenberg, *Final Freedom*, 217.
26. For a good discussion about New Jersey on the border of slavery, see Gillette, *Jersey Blue*, 1–17.
27. *Debates in the Eighty-Ninth General Assembly of the State of New Jersey*, 26, 32.
28. Ibid., 66, 68.
29. Ibid., 46–47, 52.
30. Ibid., 36–37.
31. Gillette, *Jersey Blue*, 302–3.
32. *Sermons Preached in Boston*, 15, 53.
33. Haycraft to William H. Herndon, [June 1865,] in Wilson and Davis, *Herndon's Informants*, 67–68.
34. Vorenberg, *Final Freedom*, 214.
35. *Sermons Preached in Boston*, 101–2, 170–72.
36. *Memorial of Abraham Lincoln*, 32, 37, 41, 61.
37. Hall, *Sermon*, 12–13.
38. *Memorial of Abraham Lincoln*, 93–94, 103–10, 130, 132.
39. Ibid., 138–39.
40. Ibid., 145–52.
41. *Proceedings of the Illinois State Convention of Colored Men*, 273.

42. Holzer, "Picturing Freedom," 234–35, 245–48, 252–53, 255.
43. Vorenberg, *Final Freedom*, 244–45. See also http://philadelphiaencyclopedia.org/archive/national-freedom-day/, accessed on February 28, 2014.

Conclusion

1. Foner, *Free Soil*, 40–44.
2. For recent discussions about constitutional change outside of Article V, see, for example, Amar, "Consent of the Governed"; and Ackerman, *We the People*.
3. Lincoln, "Speech at Peoria, Illinois," October 16, 1854, *CW*, 2:276; "Speech at Chicago, Illinois," July 10, 1858, ibid., 2:501; "First Inaugural Address—Final Text," March 4, 1861, ibid., 4:264–71; "Message to Congress in Special Session," July 4, 1861, ibid., 4:435; Phillips, *War for the Union*, 17, 24.
4. Lincoln, "First Debate with Stephen A. Douglas at Ottawa, Illinois," August 21, 1858, *CW*, 3:16 ("There is no reason in the world why the negro is not entitled to all the natural rights enumerated in the Declaration of Independence—the right to life, liberty, and the pursuit of happiness"); Kyvig, *Explicit and Authentic Acts*, 154–55.
5. 14 Stat. 27.
6. Benedict, "Preserving the Constitution"; Belz, *New Birth of Freedom*, 164–65.
7. Vorenberg, *Final Freedom*, 6. The cases are *Pollock v. Farmers' Loan & Trust Company*, 157 U.S. 429 (1895) (Sixteenth Amendment); *United States v. Reese*, 92 U.S. 214 (1875) and *Breedlove v. Suttles*, 302 U.S. 277 (1937) (Twenty-Fourth Amendment); and *Oregon v. Mitchell*, 400 U.S. 112 (1970) (Twenty-Sixth Amendment). The Eleventh Amendment overruled *Chisholm v. Georgia*, 2 U.S. 419 (1793).
8. Lincoln, "Address at Sanitary Fair, Baltimore, Maryland," April 18, 1864, *CW*, 7:301–2.
9. Lincoln, "Address before the Wisconsin State Agricultural Society, Milwaukee, Wisconsin," September 30, 1859, ibid., 3:478–79, 480, 482; "Annual Message to Congress," December 3, 1861, ibid., 5:52.
10. Lincoln, "Message to Congress in Special Session," July 4, 1861, ibid., 4:438; "Speech to One Hundred Sixty-sixth Ohio Regiment," August 22, 1864, ibid., 7:512.
11. Fredrickson, *Big Enough to Be Inconsistent*, 119, 112–23.
12. *United States v. Rhodes*, 27 F. Cas. 785 (Circuit Court, D. Kentucky 1866).

13. *Civil Rights Cases*, 109 U.S. 3, 20 (quotes), 22–25, 36, 43 (1883).
14. *Jones v. Alfred H. Mayer Company*, 392 U.S. 409, 439–43 (1968); *Runyon v. McCrary*, 427 U.S. 160 (1976).
15. For broad readings, see Zietlow, "Ideological Origins," 396, 452–58; and Tsesis, "Congressional Authority," 46. For a narrower reading, see McAward, "Scope"; McAward, "*McCulloch* and the Thirteenth Amendment," 1769–70; Carter, "Race, Rights, and the Thirteenth Amendment," 1319; and *Jones*, 392 U.S. at 444.
16. For citations of the law review articles to which I refer, see McAward, "*McCulloch* and the Thirteenth Amendment," footnotes 8–14 on pp. 1770–71, and Carter, "Race, Rights, and the Thirteenth Amendment," footnote 13 on pp. 1316–17. Barack Obama, "Presidential Proclamation: National Slavery and Human Trafficking Prevention Month," January 4, 2010, http://www.whitehouse.gov/the-press-office/presidential-proclamation-national-slavery-and-human-trafficking-prevention-month, accessed March 3, 2014.
17. VanderVelde, "Thirteenth Amendment of our Aspirations," 856, 859–60, 863, 864, 867; see also VanderVelde, "Labor Vision of the Thirteenth Amendment"; Pope, "Thirteenth Amendment versus the Commerce Clause," 7, 15, 25–27, 39–45, 56; and Tsesis, "Furthering American Freedom," 311, 358, 362.
18. McAward, "*McCulloch* and the Thirteenth Amendment," 1770–71, 1773–74, 1777; Tsesis, "Congressional Authority," 58; Greene, "Thirteenth Amendment Optimism," 1735; *City of Boerne v. Flores*, 521 U.S. 507 (1997).

BIBLIOGRAPHY

Cases

Breedlove v. Suttles, 302 U.S. 277 (1937)
Chisholm v. Georgia, 2 U.S. 419 (1793)
City of Boerne v. Flores, 521 U.S. 507 (1997)
Civil Rights Cases, 109 U.S. 3 (1883)
In re Turner, 24 F. Cas. 337 (Circuit Court, D. Maryland 1867)
Jones v. Alfred H. Mayer Company, 392 U.S. 409 (1968)
Opinion of the Justices, 264 A.2d 342 (Del. 1970)
Oregon v. Mitchell, 400 U.S. 112 (1970)
Pollock v. Farmers' Loan & Trust Company, 157 U.S. 429 (1895)
Runyon v. McCrary, 427 U.S. 160 (1976)
Scott v. Sandford, 60 U.S. 393 (1857)
United States v. Reese, 92 U.S. 214 (1875)
United States v. Rhodes, 27 F. Cas. 785 (Circuit Court, D. Kentucky 1866)

Manuscripts

Patrick R. Guiney Papers. Dinand Library Rare Book Room, College of the Holy Cross, Worcester, Mass.
Horace Mann Hawthorne-Mann Family Correspondence. David M. Rubenstein Rare Book and Manuscript Library, Duke University, Durham, N.C.
Abraham Lincoln Papers. Library of Congress, Washington, D.C.
William Henry Seward Papers. Department of Rare Books and Special Collections, Rush Rhees Library, University of Rochester, Rochester, N.Y.

Contemporary Periodicals

Congressional Globe
Harper's Weekly
New York Herald
Liberator
New York Times

Other Sources

Ackerman, Bruce. *We the People: Transformations*. Cambridge, Mass.: Harvard University Press, 1998.
Address of Democratic Members of Congress to the Democracy of the United States. Washington, D.C.: n.p., 1864.

Amar, Akhil Reed. "The Consent of the Governed: Constitutional Amendment outside Article V." *Columbia Law Review* 94 (1994): 457–508.

Ames, Herman V. *The Proposed Amendments to the Constitution of the United States during the First Century of Its History*. In *Annual Report of the American Historical Association for the Year 1896*. Washington, D.C.: Government Printing Office, 1897.

Arnold, Isaac N. *The History of Abraham Lincoln and the Overthrow of Slavery*. Chicago: Clarke and Co., 1866.

Baker, James H. *Lives of the Governors of Minnesota*. St. Paul: Minnesota Historical Society, 1908.

Bates, Edward. *The Diary of Edward Bates*. Edited by Howard K. Beale. Washington, D.C.: Government Printing Office, 1933.

Belz, Herman. *New Birth of Freedom: The Republican Party and Freedmen's Rights, 1861–1866*. 1976; repr., New York: Fordham University Press, 2000.

Benedict, Michael Les. "Preserving the Constitution: The Conservative Basis of Radical Reconstruction." In *Preserving the Constitution: Essays on Politics and the Constitution in the Reconstruction Era*, 3–22. New York: Fordham University Press, 2006.

Benning, Henry L. "Address of Hon. Henry L. Benning, of Georgia." In *Addresses Delivered before the Virginia State Convention by Hon. Fulton Anderson, Commissioner from Mississippi; Hon. Henry L. Benning, Commissioner from Georgia; and Hon. John S. Preston, Commissioner from South Carolina, February 1861*, 21–42. Richmond: Wyatt M. Elliott, 1861.

Blaine, James G. *Twenty Years of Congress: From Lincoln to Garfield*. 2 vols. Norwich, Conn.: Henry Bill Publishing Company, 1884.

Blair, Montgomery. *Speech of Montgomery Blair, (Postmaster General,) on the Revolutionary Schemes of the Ultra Abolitionists, and in Defence of the Policy of the President*. New York: D. W. Lee, 1863.

Bogue, Allan G. *The Earnest Men: Republicans of the Civil War Senate*. Ithaca: Cornell University Press, 1981.

Boutwell, George S. *Reminiscences of Sixty Years in Public Affairs*. 2 vols. New York: McClure, Phillips and Co., 1902.

Brooks, Noah. *Washington in Lincoln's Time*. New York: Century Co., 1896.

Burlingame, Michael, ed. *At Lincoln's Side: John Hay's Civil War Correspondence and Selected Writings*. Carbondale: Southern Illinois University Press, 2000.

———. *Lincoln Observed: Civil War Dispatches of Noah Brooks*. Baltimore: Johns Hopkins University Press, 1998.

———. *With Lincoln in the White House: Letters, Memoranda, and Other Writings of John G. Nicolay, 1860–1865*. Carbondale: Southern Illinois University Press, 2000.

Burlingame, Michael, and John R. Turner Ettlinger, eds. *Inside Lincoln's White House: The Complete Civil War Diary of John Hay*. Carbondale: Southern Illinois University Press, 1997.

Campbell, John A. *Reminiscences and Documents Relating to the Civil War during the Year 1865*. Baltimore: John Murphy and Co., 1887.

Carter, William M., Jr. "Race, Rights, and the Thirteenth Amendment: Defining the Badges and Incidents of Slavery." *UC Davis Law Review* 40, no. 4 (2007): 1311–79.

Cole, Cornelius. *The Reminiscences of a Forty-Niner: Memoirs of Cornelius Cole*. New York: McLoughlin Brothers, 1908.

"The Constitutional Amendment." *Continental Monthly*, September 1864, 315–26.

Cox, LaWanda, and John H. Cox. *Politics, Principle, and Prejudice 1865–1866*. New York: Free Press of Glencoe, 1963.

Cox, Samuel S. *Eight Years in Congress from 1857–1865*. New York: D. Appleton and Company, 1865.

———. *Union—Disunion—Reunion: Three Decades of Federal Legislation*. Providence: J. A. and R. A. Reid, Publishers, 1885.

Curtis, Benjamin R. *Executive Power*. Boston: Little, Brown and Company, 1862.

Dana, Charles A. *Recollections of the Civil War*. New York: D. Appleton and Co., 1902.

Debates in the Eighty-Ninth General Assembly of the State of New Jersey on the Bill to Ratify an Amendment to the Constitution of the United States. Trenton: J. R. Freese, 1865.

Dew, Charles B. *Apostles of Disunion: Southern Secession Commissioners and the Causes of the Civil War*. Charlottesville: University of Virginia Press, 2001.

Donald, David Herbert. *Lincoln*. New York: Random House, 1995.

Douglass, Frederick. *The Frederick Douglass Papers: Series One, Speeches, Debates and Interviews*. Edited by John W. Blassingame and John R. McKivigan. 5 vols. New Haven: Yale University Press, 1979–92.

"Exposition and Protest Reported by the Special Committee of the House of Representatives of South Carolina on the Tariff (December 19, 1828)." In *The Statutes at Large of South Carolina*, 1:247–73. Columbia, S.C.: A. S. Johnston, 1836.

Finkelman, Paul. "Lincoln, Emancipation, and the Limits of Constitutional Change." *Supreme Court Review*, 2008, 349–87.

Foner, Eric. *Free Soil, Free Labor, Free Men: The Ideology of the Republican Party before the Civil War*. New York: Oxford University Press, 1971.

Fredrickson, George M. *Big Enough to Be Inconsistent: Abraham Lincoln Confronts Slavery and Race*. Cambridge, Mass.: Harvard University Press, 2008.

Garrison, William Lloyd. *The Letters of William Lloyd Garrison*. Edited by Walter M. Merrill. 6 vols. Cambridge, Mass.: Belknap Press of Harvard University Press, 1971–81.

Gillette, William. *Jersey Blue: Civil War Politics in New Jersey, 1854–1865*. New Brunswick, N.J.: Rutgers University Press, 1995.

Goodwin, Doris Kearns. *Team of Rivals: The Political Genius of Abraham Lincoln*. New York: Simon and Schuster, 2005.

Greene, Jamal. "Thirteenth Amendment Optimism." *Columbia Law Review* 112 (2012): 1733–68.

Hall, Newman. *A Sermon on the Assassination of Abraham Lincoln Preached at Surrey Chapel, London, Sunday, May 14, 1865*. Boston: Bartlett and Halliday, 1865.

Harris, William C. *With Charity for All: Lincoln and the Restoration of the Union*. Lexington: University Press of Kentucky, 1997.

Hofstadter, Richard. *The American Political Tradition and the Men Who Made It*. New York: Vintage Books, 1961.

Holt, Michael F. *The Rise and Fall of the American Whig Party: Jacksonian Politics and the Onset of the Civil War*. New York: Oxford University Press, 1999.

Holzer, Harold. *Lincoln President-Elect: Abraham Lincoln and the Great Secession, Winter 1860–1861*. New York: Simon and Schuster, 2008.

———. "Picturing Freedom: The Thirteenth Amendment in the Graphic Arts." In *Lincoln and Freedom: Slavery, Emancipation, and the Thirteenth Amendment*, edited by Harold Holzer and Sara Vaughn Gabbard, 233–56. Carbondale: Southern Illinois University Press, 2007.

Jay, John. *Mr. Jay's Remarks at the Celebration Dinner of the East Brooklyn Union Campaign Club, at the Pierrepont House, Brooklyn, on Thursday Evening, December 22, 1864*. [New York?]: n.p., [1864].

Johnson, Andrew. *The Papers of Andrew Johnson*. 16 vols. Knoxville: University of Tennessee Press, 1989.

Julian, George W. *Political Recollections: 1840 to 1872*. Chicago: Jansen, McClurg and Company, 1884.

Keller, Ron J. "'That Which Congress So Nobly Began': The Men Who Passed the Thirteenth Amendment Resolution." In *Lincoln and Freedom: Slavery, Emancipation, and the Thirteenth Amendment*, edited by Harold Holzer and Sara Vaughn Gabbard, 195–212. Carbondale: Southern Illinois University Press, 2007.

Kyvig, David E. *Explicit and Authentic Acts: Amending the U.S. Constitution, 1776–1995*. Lawrence: University Press of Kansas, 1996.

Lee, R. Alton, "The Corwin Amendment in the Secession Crisis." *Ohio Historical Quarterly* 70 (January 1961): 1–26.

Levinson, Sanford. "Was the Emancipation Proclamation Constitutional? Do We/Should We Care What the Answer Is?" *University of Illinois Law Review* 5 (2001): 1135–58.

Lincoln, Abraham. *The Collected Works of Abraham Lincoln*. Edited by Roy P. Basler. 9 vols. New Brunswick, NJ: Rutgers University Press, 1953–55.

Lupton, John A. "Abraham Lincoln and the Corwin Amendment." At http://www.lib.niu.edu/2006/ih060934.html. Accessed January 8, 2014.

Masur, Louis P. *Lincoln's Hundred Days: The Emancipation Proclamation and the War for the Union*. Cambridge, Mass.: Harvard University Press, 2012.

McAward, Jennifer Mason. "*McCulloch* and the Thirteenth Amendment." *Columbia Law Review* 112 (2012): 1769–1809.

———. "The Scope of Congress's Thirteenth Amendment Enforcement Power after *City of Boerne v. Flores*." *Washington University Law Review* 88 (2010): 77–147.

McPherson, Edward. *A Hand-book of Politics for 1872: Being a Record of Important Political Action, National and State, from July 15, 1870, to July 15, 1872*. Washington, D.C.: Philp and Solomons, 1872.

———. *The Political History of the United States of America during the Great Rebellion*. Washington, D.C.: Philp and Solomons, 1864.

Meagher, Thomas F. *Letters on Our National Struggle, by Brig.-Gen. Thos. Francis Meagher*. New York: Loyal Publication Society, 1863.

A Memorial of Abraham Lincoln, Late President of the United States. Boston: J. E. Farwell and Company, 1865.

Neely, Mark E., Jr. *Lincoln and the Triumph of the Nation: Constitutional Conflict in the American Civil War*. Chapel Hill: University of North Carolina Press, 2011.

Nicolay, John G., and John Hay. *Abraham Lincoln: A History*. 10 vols. New York: Century Co., 1886–1890.

Official Register of Officers and Agents, Civil, Military and Naval, in the Service of the United States on the Thirtieth September, 1865. Washington, D.C.: Government Printing Office, 1866.

Oldroyd, Osborn H., ed. *The Lincoln Memorial: Album-Immortelles*. New York: G. W. Carleton and Co., 1882.

Paulsen, Michael Stokes. "The Emancipation Proclamation and the Commander in Chief Power." *Georgia Law Review* 40 (2006): 807–34.

Phillips, Wendell. *The War for the Union; A Lecture*. New York: E. D. Barker, 1862.

Pomeroy, Earl S. "Lincoln, the Thirteenth Amendment, and the Admission of Nevada." *Pacific Historical Review* 12, no. 4 (December 1943): 362–68.

Pope, James Gray. "The Thirteenth Amendment versus the Commerce Clause: Labor and the Shaping of American Constitutional Law, 1921–1957." *Columbia Law Review* 102 (2002): 1–122.

Proceedings of the First Three Republican National Conventions of 1856, 1860, and 1864, Including Proceedings of the Antecedent National Convention held at Pittsburg [sic], *in February, 1856, as Reported by Horace Greeley.* Minneapolis: Harrison and Smith, 1893.

Proceedings of the Illinois State Convention of Colored Men, Assembled at Galesburg, October 16th, 17th, and 18th [1866] (Chicago, 1867). In *Proceedings of the Black National and State Conventions, 1865–1900*, edited by Philip S. Foner and George E. Walker, 249–75. Philadelphia: Temple University Press, 1986.

Proceedings of the National Convention of Colored Men, Held in the City of Syracuse, N.Y. October 4, 5, 6, and 7, 1864; with the Bill of Wrongs and Rights and the Address to the American People. Boston: Geo. C. Rand and Avery, 1864.

Proceedings of the National Convention to Secure the Religious Amendment of the Constitution of the United States Held in New York, Feb. 26 and 27, 1873. New York: John Polhemus, Printer, 1873.

Rable, George C. *The Confederate Republic: A Revolution against Politics.* Chapel Hill: University of North Carolina Press, 1994.

Report of the Committee of Thirteen. 36th Cong., 2nd Sess., Rep. Com. No. 288.

Rhodehamel, John H., and Seth Kaller. "A Census of Copies of the Thirteenth Amendment to the U.S. Constitution Signed by Abraham Lincoln." *Manuscripts*, 44, no. 2 (Spring 1992): 93–114.

Rice, Allen Thorndike, ed. *Reminiscences of Abraham Lincoln by Distinguished Men of His Time.* New York: North American Publishing Company, 1886.

Richardson, James D., ed. *A Compilation of the Messages and Papers of the Presidents, 1789–1897.* 20 vols. New York: Bureau of National Literature, 1897.

Riddle, Albert G. *Recollections of War Times: Reminiscences of Men and Events in Washington, 1860–1865.* New York: G. P. Putnam's Sons, 1893.

Samito, Christian G. *Becoming American under Fire: Irish Americans, African Americans, and the Politics of Citizenship during the Civil War Era.* Ithaca: Cornell University Press, 2009.

Schurz, Carl. *Intimate Letters of Carl Schurz, 1841–1869.* Edited by Joseph Schafer. Madison: State Historical Society of Wisconsin, 1928.

Scovel, James M. "Thaddeus Stevens." *Lippincott's Monthly Magazine*, April 1898, 545–51.

Sermons Preached in Boston on the Death of Abraham Lincoln. Together with the Funeral Services in the East Room of the Executive Mansion at Washington. Boston: J. E. Tilton and Company, 1865.

Seward, William H. *Remarks of Hon. Wm. H. Seward, on the Occasion of the Fall of Atlanta, at Auburn, Saturday, Sept. 3, 1864*. Albany: Weed, Parsons, and Company, 1864.

Stephens, Alexander H. *A Constitutional View of the Late War Between the States*. 2 vols. Philadelphia: National Publishing Co., 1868–70.

Stevens, Thaddeus. *The Selected Papers of Thaddeus Stevens, April 1865–August 1868*. 2 vols. Edited by Beverly Wilson Palmer and Holly Byers Ochoa. Pittsburgh: University of Pittsburgh Press, 1998.

Sumner, Charles. *Our Domestic Relations: Or, How to Treat the Rebel States*. Boston, 1863.

Sylvester, Nathaniel B. *History of Rensselaer Co., New York*. Philadelphia: Everts and Peck, 1880.

Tsesis, Alexander. "Congressional Authority to Interpret the Thirteenth Amendment." *Maryland Law Review* 71 (2011): 40–59.

———. "Furthering American Freedom: Civil Rights and the Thirteenth Amendment." *Boston College Law Review* 45 (2004): 307–90.

United States Congress. *The Debates and Proceedings in the Congress of the United States*. Washington: Gales and Seaton, 1834–56. Also called the *Annals of Congress*.

———. *Statutes at Large, Treaties, and Proclamations of the United States of America*. 18 vols. Boston: Little, Brown, 1845–73; Washington: Government Printing Office, 1875–.

———. Senate. *Senate Executive Journal*. Washington: Government Printing Office, 1828–.

Usher, John P. "Abraham Lincoln: The President and His Advisors." *New York Tribune*, September 13, 1885.

VanderVelde, Lea. "The Labor Vision of the Thirteenth Amendment." *University of Pennsylvania Law Review* 138 (1989): 437–504.

———. "The Thirteenth Amendment of Our Aspirations." *University of Toledo Law Review* 38 (2007): 855–81.

Veto Messages of the Presidents of the United States, with the Action of Congress Thereon. Washington, D.C.: Government Printing Office, 1886.

Vorenberg, Michael. *Final Freedom: The Civil War, the Abolition of Slavery, and the Thirteenth Amendment*. New York: Cambridge University Press, 2001.

———. "The Thirteenth Amendment Enacted." In *Lincoln and Freedom: Slavery, Emancipation, and the Thirteenth Amendment*, edited by Harold Holzer and Sara Vaughn Gabbard, 180–94. Carbondale: Southern Illinois University Press, 2007.

Wagandt, Charles Lewis. *The Mighty Revolution: Negro Emancipation in Maryland, 1862–1864*. 1964; repr., Baltimore: Maryland Historical Society, 2004.

Walker, R. J. *Letter of Hon. R. J. Walker, in Favor of the Reelection of Abraham Lincoln, London, Sept. 30, 1864*. New York: n.p., 1864.

Welles, Gideon. *Diary of Gideon Welles*. 3 vols. Boston: Houghton Mifflin Company, 1911.

———. "The History of Emancipation." *Galaxy*, December 1872, 838–51.

Weygant, Charles H. *History of the One Hundred and Twenty-Fourth Regiment N.Y.S.V.* Newburgh, N.Y.: Journal Printing House, 1877.

Williams, Frank J. *Judging Lincoln*. Carbondale: Southern Illinois University Press, 2002.

Wilson, Douglas L., and Rodney O. Davis, eds. *Herndon's Informants: Letters, Interviews, and Statements about Abraham Lincoln*. Urbana: University of Illinois Press, 1998.

Winthrop, Robert C. *Great Speech of Hon. Robert C. Winthrop, At New London, Conn., October 18 [1864]*. New York: n.p., 1864.

Zietlow, Rebecca E. "The Ideological Origins of the Thirteenth Amendment." *Houston Law Review* 49 (2012): 393–458.

INDEX

Italicized page numbers indicate figures.

Christian G. Samito earned his law degree from Harvard Law School and his doctorate in American history from Boston College. He currently teaches legal history at Boston University School of Law and practices law in Boston. His most recent books are *Becoming American under Fire: Irish Americans, African Americans, and the Politics of Citizenship during the Civil War Era* and *Changes in Law and Society during the Civil War and Reconstruction: A Legal History Documentary Reader*.

CONCISE
LINCOLN
LIBRARY

This series of concise books fills a need for short studies of the life, times, and legacy of President Abraham Lincoln. Each book gives readers the opportunity to quickly achieve basic knowledge of a Lincoln-related topic. These books bring fresh perspectives to well-known topics, investigate previously overlooked subjects, and explore in greater depth topics that have not yet received book-length treatment. For a complete list of current and forthcoming titles, see www.conciselincolnlibrary.com.

Other Books in the Concise Lincoln Library

Abraham Lincoln and Horace Greeley
Gregory A. Borchard

Lincoln and the Civil War
Michael Burlingame

Lincoln and the Constitution
Brian R. Dirck

Lincoln and the Election of 1860
Michael S. Green

Lincoln and the Union Governors
William C. Harris

Lincoln's Campaign Biographies
Thomas A. Horrocks

Lincoln and the Military
John F. Marszalek

Lincoln and Emancipation
Edna Greene Medford

Lincoln and Reconstruction
John C. Rodrigue

Lincoln and Medicine
Glenna R. Schroeder-Lein

Lincoln and the U.S. Colored Troops
John David Smith

Lincoln's Assassination
Edward Steers, Jr.

Lincoln and Race
Richard Striner

Lincoln and Religion
Ferenc Morton Szasz with Margaret Connell Szasz

Lincoln and the War's End
John C. Waugh

Lincoln as Hero
Frank J. Williams

Abraham and Mary Lincoln
Kenneth J. Winkle